Upstairs & Downstairs

My Life In Service as a Lady's Maid

Hilda Newman

With Tim Tate

JOHN BLAKE

Published by John Blake Publishing,
The Plaza,
535 Kings Road,
Chelsea Harbour,
London SW10 0SZ

www.facebook.com/johnblakebooks
twitter.com/jblakebooks

First published in paperback by John Blake Publishing
in 2013 as *Diamonds At Dinner*.
This paperback edition first published in 2019.

Paperback ISBN: 978 1 78946 127 5
Ebook ISBN: 978 1 78219 782 9

British Library Cataloguing-in-Publication Data:

A catalogue record for this book is available from the British Library.

Design by www.envydesign.co.uk

Printed and bound in Great Britain by Clays Ltd, Elcograf S.p.A.

1 3 5 7 9 10 8 6 4 2

Publishers Note:
Hilda Newman passed away in August 2018, just before her 102nd birthday.
This edition has been published with the permission of her family.

John Blake Publishing is an imprint of Bonnier Books UK
www.bonnierbooks.co.uk

Contents

Introduction

The gateway loomed before me. Beautiful and soft seeming in the summer sunlight, but solid and strong and – from where I sat in the front seat of the little blue van – forbiddingly tall. I glanced at the older man in the driver's seat. He smiled reassuringly but I felt the butterflies growing more frantic in my stomach.

We had been driving for what seemed like an age. From Worcester railway station we quickly left the town behind, following small and empty country lanes as they wound past fields and dense woodland. I had no idea what direction we were going in – North? South? – I couldn't have told you, much less where exactly we were going to end up. We seemed to be travelling mile after mile, ever deeper into the very heart of England. For a young town girl like me the endless rolling landscape felt alien and somehow frightening. I had never seen so many fields, so much open country.

I pushed myself down lower into the van's seat, thinking of the cosy little cottage I had left behind me, of my little sister and brother, and of the mum and dad I had left – for the very first time – so many hours before. Had I ever even sat in a motorcar before? Certainly not alone with a man, and an older man to boot. I had never been so far away from home or felt so alone and isolated.

With a start the van slipped under the imposing stone arch and slowly picked up speed along a narrow and winding driveway. Huge swathes of open parkland slipped past, with a wide and sluggish watercourse running through it: did these people have their own private river? In the distance I saw stone buildings – some of them looked like the ancient Greek temples I had seen in schoolbooks – scattered randomly across the never-ending acres of the estate.

The driveway seemed to go on forever, and then, as we rounded a last bend, I saw it: a huge stone mansion in the middle of the park, bathed in the soft afternoon light. It had two impossibly tall wings on either side of a central entrance flanked by round pillars, each at least 20 feet tall. A third massive section – almost as big as the others and clearly a separate courtyard with stables – was joined to the left side of the main building. I had never seen anything so big or so grand in all my 19 years.

Introduction

This, then, was Croome Court. This vast and magnificent house was to be my new place of employment and my new home. I should have felt excited, astonished or grateful for the chance to live in such a wonderful place. Instead, as the car pulled up on the crunching gravel, I felt as if I'd gone to prison.

Chapter One

Stamford by Gaslight

I am, it is safe to say, old now. Though a more polite way of looking at it would be to say that I have seen a lot of history. I arrived in the middle of one world war and served in uniform in the second. Eighteen governments – of all sorts and political colours – and twenty different prime ministers have come and gone. I have lived through the reigns of two and a half kings (more of which later) and was ten years old before our present Queen was born. In a very few years – if both of us are spared – she will send me a telegram to celebrate my 100th birthday.

I am, I suppose, a living piece of history: my body, which has grown old and frail, has registered the passing of ages, as a fossil captures and preserves its times for generations to come. But my mind, well, that's still as sharp as ever; still able to conjure up the memories and images of an era – more than one, perhaps – taught to my great-grandchildren in school history lessons.

And so I have a story to tell. And you, readers, why do you look within? Have you seen *Downton Abbey* or *Upstairs Downstairs* and come in search of stories from inside the aristocracy? Good: you shall not be disappointed, for there is much I have to tell you of life with the Earl and Countess of Coventry – one of the oldest and greatest families in the land – and of the lives that played out both above and below stairs at Croome Court, one of the grandest houses in England, set amid the rolling fields of Worcestershire. This, to be sure, is a tale of the gentry and of a leisured existence long since blown away by the coming of a new world.

Perhaps, though, you want a little more than this servant's-eye-view: perhaps you have a sense that television dramas, all fine and good as may be, aren't the whole story. Maybe you seek a different tale, one which shows the grit as well as the glamour: if so, you are doubly welcome, for my story is not simply that of a servant in a great house.

It is a story both of the times and of its time. It is a story of the rich and powerful and the ordinary folk who served them; it is the story of a mansion – and oh, what a mansion. But it is also the story of the smaller, meaner homes of ordinary people. Perhaps it will serve to remind you – to remind us all – where we once came from and how we once lived. And that is important for, if we forget – or if we never knew – where we have come from, how will we know who we really are? If we lose touch with our history – rich and poor, grand and humble – how can we feel settled in ourselves? Without our stories – perhaps without my story – we, the people, will lose sight of our country and how we came to be.

If the past is another country, its gatekeepers are those who are steadily passing into the night, who have lived and breathed and survived it. And so my own story must be told soon for, as I have said, I am old – 97 now – and time will soon take me and my memories away and, with me, one more small piece of the jigsaw puzzle of our country – of our life – will be lost.

I shall tell you a story that began long, long ago and of which I am the living proof. I have the feeling that this will be the last time I tell this tale, so be comfortable, be patient and, if my memory fails sometimes or plays the tricks that come with and plague advancing years, well, then, you will, I hope, forgive an old lady who has much on her mind. From my heart I shall tell you my story and I shall speak true and with the kindness – if not the wisdom! – that seeps its way into old bones.

To begin our story we must venture not to the rural folds of Worcestershire, nor to a great country house. Our journey begins in a small, quiet town in Lincolnshire and – to be specific – in the close confines of the front room of a tiny red-bricked cottage in Red Lion Square in Stamford.

The year is 1916. Britain has been at war with Germany for two long and bloody years. Two harsh winters and two balmy summers have passed since hundreds of thousands of brave young men left their homes for the squalid and blood-flooded trenches of France. Many have already been consumed by the industrialised carnage of Flanders, never to return to till England's fields or labour in its factories.

But my father has been lucky. He has not been claimed by the mass slaughter of Mons or Ypres or the Somme. And that August he is about to receive a letter, addressed to him care of his regiment, somewhere in France. All letters to and from Tommies in France were subject to censorship – a little blue pencil wielded by an unknown official in the War Office in London. Perhaps fearing this, my mother has devised a code of her own to deliver some important news. 'The cushion has arrived. It does not have a tassel.'

Quite what the censor must have made of this cryptic message we cannot know. But my father understood it straight away. His first child – me – had been born. And as to the tassel? Well, little girls don't have 'tassels', do they?

It can't have been easy for my parents, those first two years: Dad, away at the front with the concerns and yearnings that any new father has, added to the daily – often nightly – terrors of the First World War. He must, too, have feared greatly that his 'number might come up'; that he might, as they used to say in the trenches, 'go west' before he ever had the chance to see or hold me. Perhaps he sometimes wondered whether he would be lucky enough to 'cop a Blighty' – be wounded sufficiently badly to be shipped home. That would, at least, ensure he lived and would know me, even at the cost of some terrible injury.

For Mum, too, those first two years of my life must have been terribly difficult. She was a young mother alone with a new baby in a tiny terraced cottage and constantly worrying about her husband. It was, I know, a plight endured by thousands of women in those dark times but we forget, I think, how primitive communication was back then. Mum would have received no news of Dad in the ways we take for granted now: telephones were few and far between – the privilege of the rich, or reserved for businesses that couldn't function without them. There was no television, of course, and the BBC hadn't even been established. Newspaper reports were the only way families could find out anything about the war but they were heavily censored and days, if not weeks, out of date.

I am immensely proud to introduce you to my parents because, whatever the hardships of those times – and we'll come to those, I promise – my Mum and Dad were the best parents a girl could ever hope for. They may not have had much money but they were 'respectable poor': they had standards, which they stuck to throughout their lives and instilled into their family. Later I would look back on these strong, principled working-class people and wonder at the behaviour of those who society had placed above them – at least in terms of money and standing – and wonder why the rich and privileged didn't seem to have the same values as those they looked down on.

Robert Mulley was my dad. He was born in 1886 – a year before Queen Victoria celebrated her Golden Jubilee – in a tiny village called Elmswell in the middle of Suffolk. He trained to be an engineer – a very good and skilled job in those days. At some point – I've never known why – he travelled the 80 miles to Stamford.

In those days this would be quite a journey and not one that most people of our class would ever do: working people in the 19th century tended to stay put. People were born, lived and died in a village or town and rarely, if ever, ventured further than a few miles. There were no cars, nor any buses, and a train journey would involve any number of changes and be quite expensive. So Dad must have had some reason for coming halfway across the country.

Maybe it was work that brought him to Stamford for, by the time he met my Mum – Hilda Annie Blake, as she then was – he was employed at the town's biggest engineering company, Blackstone's. They married at All Saints Church, right in the centre of Stamford, in 1913, less than a year before the outbreak of the Great War. Their first home – and the place where I was born – was no more than a cock-stride across the square from the church.

Right next door to our little house was The Crown Hotel. One of Mum's sisters – I had two maternal aunts, Beat and Chris – had a job there and, in the years to come, that position would prove very important indeed for our family. It also must have made life a little easier for Mum in the two years between my birth and Dad coming home from the war.

I'm very happy to say Dad came back safe and sound: and if, like all the men of that time who had served in the army and experienced the terrible ordeal of that most terrible war, he must have suffered mentally, at least he never lost a limb or suffered a life-threatening injury.

The great promise – made by the high and mighty in the government – was that, for men like Dad, Britain would be 'a home fit for heroes'. Well, that's the thing about politicians' promises: it's all jam tomorrow. Because, when Dad came home, he had no job to go back to at Blackstone's. And in those days, no job meant no money:

there was precious little in the way of welfare, even for returning war heroes – and, anyway, most people who had any choice in the matter had too much pride to go cap in hand for what was thought of as 'charity'.

So Dad set himself up in a little business of his own as a boot and shoe repairer. To be sure, it didn't bring a whole lot in the way of money into the house but Dad worked hard to see that his family had enough to eat. And when times were harder than normal, Mum's sister found him work at the Crown Hotel – not behind the bar (back then serving alcoholic drinks was not always viewed as the most respectable of occupations) but as a 'boots'. Every self-respecting hotel had one of these in those days: the 'boots' was responsible for cleaning and polishing the shoes that guests left outside their room at night, and making sure that they were neatly lined up, spick and span and shining, so you could see your face in them when they opened the door again the next morning.

In 1918 my sister Joan was born and, two years later, she was followed by a little brother, Jim. There were now five of us in the little two-bedroom terraced house in Red Lion Square and it was time to find somewhere larger. These days so many people, when they're married and have a family, take it for granted that they will buy a home of their own. But in the 1920s – and for decades to come – it would never have occurred to us: owning

the River Welland, flowing out to the North Sea, and ensured the success of its trade. By the 13th century Stamford was one of the 10 largest towns in England. It had a castle, 14 churches, 2 monasteries and 4 separate friaries. Parliaments met here and there was a tradition of academic learning which finally led, in the mid-14th century, to the establishment of a short-lived university.

In the 16th century Stamford was really put on the map when one of the local gentry, William Cecil, became Queen Elizabeth the First's Secretary of State. She pretty swiftly created a whole new hereditary peerage for him: the first Baron Burghley (as Cecil became) built himself a palatial mansion just outside the town and became the main owner of houses within it. I can't be certain but I think the house I grew up in was owned by his descendants: if so, it could have been a sign, pointing the way to the life I would lead as an adult. When the English Civil War tore England apart, the fugitive King Charles hid out at Burghley House and Oliver Cromwell laid siege to it. But the rest of the town got off fairly lightly.

Because of its position, anyone who travelled north from London had to pass through Stamford and the coaching trade elevated old medieval inns into major nationally renowned hostelries. Soon, prosperous professional men and merchants were attracted to the town and they built their fine houses, which have lasted until today, as well as the more humble homes constructed for their workers – and in which I would be born.

The arrival of the railway in the 1830s signalled a death-blow to the coaching trade and, with it, Stamford's fortunes. The main train line to the north bypassed the town and so stunted industrial development. But Stamford people were made of stern stuff: they adapted to the industrial revolution and quickly became famous as skilled agricultural engineers. Blackstone's, the factory where my Dad worked before he went off to war, was just one of the companies which set up and prospered.

But the railway's bypassing of Stamford would have a much longer-lasting – and, ultimately, much more pleasant – result. The fact that it escaped the vast satanic mills and shoddy terraces of mean workers' hovels, which broke out like sores in other places – together with the traditional, almost feudal, relationship between the ordinary people and the aristocracy – preserved and pickled our little town in history. The very streets where I grew up living and playing were unchanged from a century or more before and they're still like that – on the outside at least – today. Which is why, almost 80 years after I was born, the BBC chose Stamford as the place to film its great Victorian drama serial *Middlemarch*.

Now, I said that the houses – including our little home at Number 5, Vine Street – remain just the same on the outside, and so they do. But if you want to know about life – real, honest, working-class life – in the 1920s and 1930s, we must step inside. And how different things are here. Let's open the front door – which led directly into the front room – and step back into history.

As you read this, please look around your home and see all the everyday things we now take for granted in our lives. Not just the television and DVD player; the computers, connected to the whole world via the Internet; the telephones – both mobile and plugged into the wall; the washing machine and the microwave oven. No – look again and try to see with my old eyes the things that, as a child, would have seemed like something out of science fiction (if that term had even been invented). You may be reading this with the lights on. Today we never even stop to think about flicking a switch when it gets dark. But there was no electricity in Number 5, Vine Street: in the 1920s very few houses – not even many of the grand and magnificent mansions of the gentry, and certainly not the sort of humble houses that working-class people lived in – were wired for electric power. For us, turning the light on was something only grown-ups could do, because our lamps were powered by gas.

If that seems archaic to you, we were one of the lucky families: many – perhaps most – people of my class at that time lit their homes with paraffin lamps. And the reason only an adult could turn on the lamps in our house was because you had to be careful with gas. It was piped to the light in copper tubes, which stretched up the walls and across the ceiling: a little brass tap regulated the supply. The lamps themselves had a small net bag – known as a mantle – made of cotton impregnated with metal: the gas was forced through this and had to be lit with a burning taper. It would make a popping sound when the flame met the gas and gave off a slightly sickly yellow glow. Often as not the mere act of lighting it or (more often) turning the gas off at the tap would cause a small explosion, which blew the mantle into tiny bits. Replacing it meant a trip to the ironmonger's shop and then fiddling about for an age to fit the new one in place. Sometimes today, when a light bulb blows in my nicely lit flat and a fresh one has to be popped in, I remember just how awkward and time consuming it was just to get the lamps working in those long-ago days and nights.

From the front room, come with me to the kitchen. With no electricity there was, of course, no fridge (let alone a freezer): no one – neither rich nor poor – had anything that would be recognised as a fridge until after the Great War. The earliest models were nothing but wooden cabinets with ice slowly melting in the top. Then, in the 1920s, came the first true fridges, which generated cold by compressing gases, just as ours do today. The catch was that the original refrigerants were toxic – and, of course, they were so expensive that only the very few could afford them. Since electricity was also a rarity in houses, some companies tried out gas-powered fridges, marketing them as 'modern marvels of the age'. But they, too, cost a small fortune; the vast majority of the population wouldn't own a refrigerator until the early 1960s.

Instead, we had a larder. This was a narrow room off the kitchen with a big stone shelf. Because the larder was on an outside wall, with a rectangular hole covered with a perforated iron plate, the stone shelf stayed cold and perishable food was placed on it to keep fresh. Of course, it wouldn't last long, so Mum would go shopping almost every day – and in the days before supermarkets or convenience stores that meant a lengthy trek, with me, Joan and Jim in tow, around the butchers, the bakers and (for all I can remember) the candlestick makers.

There was, of course, another reason why this rather basic system worked: the house was, invariably, cold. Today I don't think there's a home in the country that doesn't have some kind of central heating but back then it was completely unthinkable. Why? Because we didn't have any hot water.

The kitchen sink did have a tap – and in that, unlike many, we were fortunate. But the only way of heating water was in big pans on the copper boiler in the corner of the kitchen, which was heated by a coal fire. This, of course, had another implication: getting washed. All of us grew up with a morning and night-time wash in a bowl of cold water – even in the bitterest of winters. The only time we'd see hot water for washing was on a Friday night when Mum would unhook the big copper bath from the toilet wall, put it in front of the coal fire in the living room and fill it up with panful after panful, ladled one by one from the boiler. As the eldest, I'd get to go first, followed by Joan and then Jim – poor Jim; he always got the coldest and dirtiest bath! And that would be that for another week: Mum would hang the bath back in the toilet and we'd be back to a quick lick and a promise in cold water, morning and night.

Now, the toilet. It possibly won't surprise you to know that this wasn't in the house. At the end of the yard there was a little brick shed and inside was a very basic loo. Whatever the weather, whatever the time of day, if we needed to go, we'd have to nip out the back door and scuttle into the outside privy. And in winter we'd definitely scuttle quickly: there was no heating in the toilet – I'm not even sure there was a light: why would there be when there was no heating in the house itself, other than the coal fire? So we didn't linger longer than was absolutely necessary.

In case you think we were unusual or deprived in this – don't! Most of the population of Britain in those days had an outside toilet and this persisted well into the 1950s. Certainly nobody we knew had a nice warm loo in their house. That was just the way life was back then.

But we did have something special in the house – something not many other people of our class had. In the front room we had a piano. It was one of those old upright ones that you used to see in pubs in those days. And Mum and Dad were keen that I learned to play: from a very young age I was sent to have lessons – in itself, this was a luxury and I don't know how Mum found the money from her limited weekly housekeeping. Luckily, I took to the piano very well: I was happy to study and practise and take all the exams so that I ended up as a pretty competent player. That's when Mum and Dad got their reward for all those costly lessons. If anyone came to visit us, I was called on to play. I didn't sing; I was too shy for that and, anyway, Dad had a lovely big voice. I would accompany him as he sang the songs he'd learned in the army during the war – good songs, they were, filled with the passion that fighting brings and the yearning for home that comes when you're far away and stuck in some terrible trench in the mud and blood of a Flanders field. 'Kiss Me Goodnight, Sergeant Major', 'When This Lousy War Is Over' and not forgetting 'It's A Long Way To Tipperary': they were good songs, those, with words and tunes that everybody knew. And if Dad didn't sing, I'd perform light classical instrumentals like 'The Blue Danube' waltz.

That was how people entertained themselves back then. There was – of course – no television and no radio: even when the BBC started regular broadcasts, very few people could afford the price of a wireless. So we made our own entertainment and it was, to my mind, a good thing: it was something that the whole family did together. That's something I think we've lost in our modern age with all its instant gratification and technological advances – and I think families are the poorer for it. I'm a big believer in the importance of family life and it makes me sad to see how much we've lost of the warmth and togetherness that was once the norm for children and their parents.

I don't remember having many books in the house as a child – but then families like us wouldn't have been able to afford them. There weren't paperbacks in those days – they didn't come along till much later – and, though I did enjoy reading, if I ever wanted a book, it had to come from Stamford's library.

This, then, was life for the Mulley family in our little home in Vine Street in the 1920s. We lived simply, as people of our class did, and there was a pattern to the week, which never varied. Monday was washing day. Mum would scrub the clothes in the kitchen sink – the washing machine was a relatively new invention – the first motor-driven wringer-washers (as they were known) had only arrived in 1911 and they were far too expensive for ordinary folk. On top of which, they were powered by electricity – and who had that in their houses in the 1920s? No one that we knew! Friday was the day when everyone ate fish: it's one of the oldest traditions in this country – in the world, in fact – dating back many hundreds of years to when Catholics were required to abstain from meat on that day. I don't suppose that in our modern, multi-faith or even secular country many people even remember the tradition, much less stick to it. But when I was growing up, no matter what branch of Christianity you came from (and we weren't Catholic), people all over England followed the practice almost without thinking. In any event, if we'd ever paused to think about it, there would have been nothing odd about abstaining from meat on a Friday: for a working-class family like ours, meat was pretty much reserved for Sunday. The Sunday roast was the great family tradition up and down the land and for very many people it would be the one and only day when meat was eaten. If you were lucky, there might enough left over to serve up in a variety of inventive ways for the man of the house on a Monday. But for me, the real treat wasn't any leftover scraps from the roast itself; it was the dripping.

Do you – does anyone – still eat bread and dripping, I wonder? It was a staple of the British diet for all my childhood but I haven't seen or heard of it for more years than I care to remember. Yet when I think about it, my mouth begins to water and I'm transported back to the tasty pleasures of a big slice of rich – and very fatty – dripping, smeared on a doorstep of good fresh bread. Delicious.

I hope you're getting the sense from all this of what life was like in those long-ago days when the last century was still new. It's a bit of a cliché, I know, but life then was much slower and still revolved around the old rhythms of the country. Spring for planting, the summer for ripening, harvest in the autumn and then the long, cold months of winter. England had, of course, been transformed by the industrial revolution but my generation was, I think, one of the last to grow up within the framework of the old rural calendar and, as a child, one of my favourites was Lent, for that was when the fair came to town.

Fairs are a very visual and telling example of how things have changed. Today, I know, fairs still travel the land and people still flock to them. But they are brash, noisome affairs today. In my childhood there were no fancy fairground rides, alive with flashing lights and pounding pop music: for us, the fair brought the exoticism of coconut shies, throwing mops at Aunt Sally – a figure of an old woman with a ruddy face and a clay pipe in her mouth, set upon a spike, that you had to knock down with rough wooden balls. But my favourite of all was the carousel – a huge, steam-driven merry-go-round with gaily coloured horses: it was the nearest I ever got to riding a real horse and I loved it.

There was another reason that we lived much more by the restrictions of the seasons then. Very few places had much in the way of street lighting and, when darkness fell, most people knew that it made sense to be indoors. Today we take well-lit streets for granted but in 1920s Stamford what few lamp posts existed were topped with gas lamps. These gave out a slightly eerie, flickering yellow-green glow, which created pools of sickly light along the pavement. They worked on the same principle as the lamps that lit our home but with one exception: the lamplighter.

Every evening just before it got dark a man on a bicycle pedalled through the streets, in one hand clutching a long wooden pole, which stretched back over his shoulder, while steering his bike with the other hand. It was his job to turn on all the street lamps and he would stop at each one in turn and reach up with his pole to turn on the gas. He would insert the pole into a hole at the bottom of the glass case and push a lever to the 'on' position. A small pilot light inside the enclosure then lit the gas, making the mantle glow. Gas street lamps like this were the norm in every sizeable town and, if they didn't give off the brightest light, at least they provided regular employment for someone. And employment, as we shall see, was becoming in short supply.

When I come to think about it, my only real experience of electricity as a child, or even a teenager (not that anyone had even heard that word back then), was at the picture house. Going to the 'flicks' – and Stamford had three 'Kinemas', all doing good business – was the closest we came to the big world outside our quiet little existence: a tantalising glimpse into how people very different to us lived their lives. I suppose the film industry must have been very young then and the pictures we saw would seem laughably primitive to a modern audience. There weren't even talkies until I was 11 years old when Warner Bros released *The Jazz Singer* in 1927 – the first movie with a soundtrack (and even this was only in parts of the film!). The standard fare was relatively short black-and-white melodramas with on-screen captions instead of dialogue. It's all light years away from today's Hollywood output but, to me, it was a window to a glittering, exciting new world. Little did I dream that in a few short years I would find myself in the very heart of somewhere much, much more glamorous.

Chapter Two

Scandal and Renaissance

The projector whirs and clicks. The screen flickers into life. A caption – curly black-and-white script against a backdrop of pillars and statues – appears: '60 Years of Happiness. Earl and Countess of Coventry celebrate their Diamond Wedding, felicitated by tenantry and relatives.'

A very old man, a shiny top hat above a round, smiling face covered in huge white whiskers, emerges from a great mansion house, his wife in the full skirts and corsetry of the Edwardian age and a clergyman in a long white cassock. Carefully and with much huffing and puffing, he is seated on a wooden chair in front of the imposing front entrance. Cut to a small army of men and women, clad in domestic uniforms and plainly the servants of the house.

The clergyman presents the old man with a scroll or paper of some kind.

The kindly looking old gentleman is the ninth Earl of Coventry. The great house is Croome Court, in the rolling heartlands of Worcestershire: the place that will – though I don't yet know it – become my home.

The film itself was a Pathé Newsreel from 1925. In those days before television news bulletins, picture houses up and down the country would screen a silent ten-minute newsreel before the showing of the main picture: this was the only way ordinary people got to see images of people and places far away from their own hometowns. Pathé was the main creator and provider of these early news films, and the Earl and Countess of Coventry were often its subjects. In 1930, five years after Pathé joined in the celebrations for the Coventry's Diamond Wedding, its cameras returned to Croome Court to mark with reverence the ninth Earl's death.

'A Grand Old English Gentleman!' the opening caption announced. 'The Earl of Coventry, one of the greatest figures of [the] English Turf, typical old English Squire & Sportsman, passes away in his 92nd year.' The film then shows the same ruddy face, still supporting enormous whiskers, grinning with happiness a few weeks earlier as he greets and shakes hands with his tenant farmers. It then cuts to the front of Croome Court and images of a pack of hunting hounds swarming and barking in front of the front entrance, before switching back to a valedictory shot of the Earl.

Today the death of a country aristocrat would never be deemed newsworthy: it might possibly make a small paragraph buried deep in the later pages of the *Daily Telegraph* but I can't imagine it being even noticed by a television news bulletin. Yet there it was in 1930 – important enough for a camera crew to be dispatched to Worcestershire from London, and to be showcased to mass audiences in cinemas up and down the land. How times change.

The Coventry family came to Croome – a shallow if large area of marshland in the valley between the rivers Severn and Avon in Worcestershire – in the later years of the 16th century. Queen Elizabeth I was still on the throne when Thomas Coventry, a successful and wealthy provincial lawyer, set about looking for a suitable piece of land to purchase as an investment. At first glance, Croome must have seemed an unlikely prospect: it was boggy, unpromising and its soil largely unworked. But a sizeable area of land to the north of Croome was already owned and farmed by his wife, and Thomas spotted the area's position – within a day's horse ride to the then prosperous city of Worcester and its satellite market towns of Pershore and Upton – and its proximity to the vital trade artery of the Severn made it much more appealing than first impressions would suggest.

There is little else of interest to record about this first

Coventry of Croome but, from the next generation onwards, the family would become very important indeed. Thomas Coventry (junior) followed in his father's legal footsteps and rose through the ranks of provincial solicitor gentlemen to become the Recorder of London and then Solicitor-General to the first of the new Stuart monarchs, King James I. In 1621 he became the MP for nearby Droitwich and, four years later, he ascended to hold the greatest of royal offices – Lord Keeper of the Great Seal of England, the priceless artefact, inscribed with the King's name, and which is used to stamp a wax imprint on all the monarch's official documents.

After James died, his son Charles I continued to favour Thomas and in 1629 he made him the first Baron of Coventry. A baronry is the lowest rank of the peerage and by 1697, when the Stuart dynasty had been replaced by the House of Hannover (and Thomas's descendant had become the 5th Baron of Coventry), the new King William rewarded the family's prominence and service to the Crown by upgrading the title to that of an earldom – the third highest rank in the nobility.

Croome Court, too, had undergone at least two rebuilds by the time the 6th Earl, George William Coventry, took up residence in the middle of the 17th century. But, to the new owner's eyes, Croome appeared dowdy, old-fashioned and unfittingly provincial in style. Apparently, he took one look and declared it 'as hopeless a spot as any on this island'. Determined to create something to rival the finest in the land, he commissioned the most fashionable architect of the day – and one of the most celebrated in English history – Lancelot Capability Brown, to create an entirely new estate with the express purpose of exciting the amazement and admiration of his peers.

Brown decided that the new Croome estate should appear to be a completely natural swathe of parkland. But to achieve this would require extraordinary feats of engineering. Acre upon acre of the land had to be drained; miles of culverts had to be constructed to carry away the unwanted water and an enormous lake with an artificial river (designed to appear as if it had always existed) had to be created.

By the time all of this landscaping work had finished Croome was transformed into one of the most impressive aristocratic estates anywhere in England. So much so that in 1792 *The Gentleman's Magazine* (can you imagine seeing such a title today?) was moved to report,

Never did I see a more beautiful spot; nor any kept in such perfect order. A vast extent of ground, formerly a mere bog, is now adorned with islands and with tufts of trees of every species; and watered round, in the most pleasing, and natural manner, possible.

But it wasn't just the parkland that got this amazing makeover. At the same time as Capability Brown was working his magic on the landscape, the 6th Earl of Coventry hired Robert Adam – the finest interior designer of the age – to renovate the main house and its numerous outbuildings. Out went all the hodge-podge of the original 16th-century fixtures and fittings; in their place Adam built magnificent neo-classical pillars and frontages and fireplaces. Actually, if you go to any DIY store today and look at ready-built fireplaces for your own home, you'll find that many are copies of the style that Adam used at Croome Court.

Not content with that – and goodness knows how much this landscaping alone must have cost the Earl – Adam was also commissioned to come up with Gothic designs for the decoration of Croome Church. Those were the days when every respectable aristocratic family had their own church built on their estate. Croome Church was built on a little hill overlooking the main house. It was a place that I came to know well and, if you wish to visit today, it's still standing, as calm and reassuring as ever – though, as we shall see, amid its lasting memorials to the dead, there lies the sad and telling outcome of a scandal.

By the time the 6th Earl died in 1809, bills for work at Croome were running at £20,000 per year – many millions of pounds in today's money. On top of that, a new window tax had been introduced. This did exactly what it

Apparently, the Viscount was a thoroughly impetuous man – he had already managed to shoot himself in the leg – and had forced his poor mount to jump a difficult five-bar gate. The horse slipped and fell on top of him with such tremendous force that – according to reports in the newspapers – his right eye 'was beat into his head, his nose broke and laid flat to his face'. As a result, he completely lost his sight and, by the time he ascended to the title 7th Earl of Coventry and returned to Croome, he was completely unable to enjoy the visual feast that his father had created on the estate. Perhaps this was one reason he caused so much anger – in the family and with his tenants – by ordering the felling of a huge number of trees on the estate. He further alienated the poor ordinary people who lived and worked at Croome by doubling their rents.

The other parts of the Coventry family spent much of the early and middle years of Queen Victoria's reign mired in scandal – more elopements, bankruptcies and a scandalous court case in which the mother of a suitor for one of the 7th Earl's daughters sued the Coventrys in the High Court in London for the Earl's refusal to allow the marriage. Meanwhile, his son, styled Lord Deerhurst and the future 8th Earl, had carried on the family tradition of a dissolute early life before eloping to Scotland with his paramour – Lady Mary Beauclerk, a descendant of King Charles II and Nell Gwynne. She appears to have been just as wild and irresponsible as her husband, having not one but two affairs shortly after their marriage – both with the future Earl's own brothers.

He promptly had a nervous breakdown, followed by Lady Mary embarking on yet another adulterous affair with one Colonel Sanders of Lee Bridge in Kent. Sanders decided to blackmail Deerhurst over his wife's philandering – a situation made even worse when Lady Mary gave birth to an illegitimate child. The upshot of all of this was a very public divorce, something truly scandalous in Victorian times. In the 19th century husbands and wives were expected to stand by each other in public, whatever either of them got up to in private.

Divorces did happen but it's certainly true that they were essentially reserved for the nobs and snobs: certainly no one of my family's class would ever have entertained the thought of divorce because of the very real social stigma that came with it. I suppose the very fact of being an aristocrat somehow insulated the gentry from this stigma.

The 8th Earl then developed a very odd reputation for meanness. Newspapers of the day had already decided he was fair game for satire and ridicule and they reported gleefully that he bought all of his clothes from second-hand shops and claimed that he dined with his tenants – the poor farm workers on the estate – six days out of seven. One such report stated, 'How noble it is to find a Peer of the Realm, possessing his thirty thousands a year, dining off a rasher of bacon and preferring that rasher at another's expense!' While a subsequent report of what in other circumstances would have been seen as a normal act of civic duty by a local landowner was turned about to become a savage satire:

This is certainly the age of wonders. It is said that the leopard cannot change its spots, but we must now believe the contrary. Dinner was lately held at Tewkesbury among the new Corporation, and we are told that 'the Earl of Coventry kindly presented the venison'. Are we to believe that he presented the venison free gratis and all for nothing? Is it likely, we ask, that this man, the meanest of the mean among the aristocracy, would give away a haunch of venison, when he will not allow any one of his own brothers, relatives or acquaintances – for friends he cannot have – to take away a single head of game from the grounds on which it is shot? The presenting of venison by Lord Coventry is about as liberal and gratifying as the presenting of a bill by one determined to sue you, if it be not paid.

The Earl sought solace from this public ridicule in a string of completely unsuitable – and, in their own way, scandalous – affairs, including a number of local working-class women and an opera singer. These liaisons produced a number of illegitimate children, with resulting demands for large sums of money to ensure their upkeep and education. The chaotic state of his personal life was reflected in a series of wills. He tore the first one to pieces in 1836, made a second four years later in which he left most of his wealth to his housekeeper, and a third one bequeathed an annuity to a mysterious Fanny Brunton, of whom his family had no knowledge whatsoever.

The 8th Earl's life was blighted with conflict, public ridicule and personal tragedy. His eldest son, who was heir to the Coventry title, had been publicly labelled a simpleton and lived a somewhat dissolute and wasteful life before being shot in the eye in a bizarre hunting accident in 1836. Two years later he attended a party held by Queen Victoria, caught a severe cold and died within weeks – thus predeceasing his father. It would not be the last time that the heir to the Coventry name passed away before inheriting.

The upshot of all this was that, when the 8th Earl finally died in 1843 – still being lampooned in the press and abused in Parliament – his successor was just five years old. It really wasn't an auspicious start and anyone looking on from outside would have viewed the succession as just the latest twist in what had become a very public soap opera.

But the 9th Earl – that kindly old bewhiskered gentleman we saw in the Pathé Newsreels at the start of this chapter – was to be the saving of the Coventry family. He would restore its good name – if not its fortunes – and once again earn for the Earldom the respect of rich and poor alike. Which is probably just as well because, if he hadn't, I can't imagine my father would have allowed me to take employment at Croome Court.

Born in 1838, George William Coventry had been brought up on the Seizincote Estate in Gloucestershire but he visited Croome Court regularly and was determined to restore it – and the family name – to its former glory. He would be the first Earl in many generations to take seriously the responsibilities that came with being one of the leading aristocratic families in England, as well as reaping its rewards.

Because he was only a child when the 8th Earl died, the estate was looked after by his great-uncle but, when the law allowed him to come into his inheritance – it was 21 before a man became legally an adult in those days – he set about his task with gusto. The Coventrys had once been one of the most respectable families in the land, with a great tradition of public service. The 9th Earl became, in fairly quick succession, the elected president of the MCC – the Marylebone Cricket Club, the foremost sporting organisation in England – a member of the Privy Council, which advised Queen Victoria on the exercise of her Royal Prerogative, and Captain and Gold Stick of the Corps of Gentleman-at-Arms, which is less formally known as the monarch's bodyguard. On top of all that, he was Lord Lieutenant of Worcestershire and a Colonel in the Worcestershire Regiment.

He also restored two other family traditions. He became a Justice of the Peace and served as chairman of the Worcestershire County Quarter Sessions (as court schedules were known back then), and he re-established the Coventry family link with hunting, serving Her Majesty as Master of The Queen's Buckhounds and Master of the newly formed North Cotswold Hunt. It was this involvement with fox hunting that would later play a leading role in the relationship between his family and me.

But as well as all this public service and polishing up of the family name amid the rich and powerful gentry, the 9th Earl also began repairing the damage his predecessors had done in relations with the ordinary working-class people who worked for him and lived on the estate.

I've always been a strong believer in two things: family and community. The 9th Earl appears to have shared my commitment: community, in particular, was very important to him and his family and they threw themselves wholeheartedly into many local causes.

One great tradition that he and his wife, Blanche, began was an act of great kindness, which marked the beginning of the Christmas festivities at Croome – and one which carried on during my time there. On Christmas Eve every year the Earl and his wife handed out gifts of beef and bread to all the tenants and their children. One such typical occasion, recorded in notes from 1915, shows that 270 large loaves, 100 small ones and 'two fat beasts' were distributed among the 167 families who lived and worked on the estate. Now, that may not sound like much to you but, in those long-ago days, such generosity from an Earl to his subjects (as I suppose we must call them) was pretty much unheard of. And in years to come it would prove a vital lifeline when times grew hard all over England.

Nor was it just a question of charity. Lord Coventry also saw that his tenants needed help in earning enough money for themselves and so he established a jam-and-pickle factory in a former industrial building, a few miles away near Pershore railway station. This enabled his tenants to sell their produce at fair market prices, thereby saving the cost of railway carriage and the risk of sending large consignments of perishable goods on long journeys. According to his diary, the factory cost £700 to build – the equivalent today of around £150,000 – and processed fruit from more than 60,000 strawberry plants, raspberry canes and currant bushes from the Croome estate.

I suppose in these cynical days, people might look on all of this and denounce the Earl as a rich paternalistic landowner, spreading a few crumbs from his lavish table on the poor and hard done by. But it wasn't like that back then and I have every reason to believe that the great tradition of Coventry benevolence that he re-established was genuine and came from his heart.

On the day he came into his inheritance, the Earl promised that he was 'ardently attached to the country, and should be pleased to spend [my] days in the midst of an affectionate tenantry'. And it seems that his tenants did genuinely love and respect him for his diligence in restoring honour to Croome Court.

And what times and glamour they must have seen. The Court regularly hosted royalty – the Prince of Wales, who would go on to become King Edward VII; the Duke and Duchess of York (the future King George V and Queen Mary, whose coronation I would one day witness for myself); the cream of European royalty and Prime Ministers and leading politicians: all of them came to house parties and country weekends in the great mansion at Croome.

The complement of servants then – the staff I would one day join – was enormous: 40 men and women – some of them really no more than children, since the lowliest servants, the hall boy and the steward's-room boy went into service at the age of 14. It was a mark of just how grand an important Croome Court was in the hierarchy of English aristocratic life: most great houses of the time employed no more than 15 servants but Croome … well, Croome was one of the greatest of the great and no expense was spared on ensuring that the Coventry family were waited on hand and foot.

As well as the wages this paid – wages which were hard-won and desperately needed in the grim years that followed the Great War – the 9th Earl was determined that his servants should be the best looked after in the land. And so he began a number of improvements to the house, improvements for which I would become deeply grateful in the years to come.

Do you remember I said that electricity was something of a rarity in those days? Like even the most humble houses – like my parent's little terraced cottage in Stamford – Croome Court was largely lit by gas. But, gradually, electric lighting was fitted in the family's quarters and in the great receptions rooms on the ground floor. Although electric lights weren't installed in the servants' bedrooms or 'beneath stairs', where most of them worked, the electrification of the house would soon bring enormous benefits to my working day.

He also commissioned a vast new furnace, fuelled by coke, which would provide hot water and – as a by-product – pump out gas to fire the remaining lights. In part, this was born of financial necessity – the 9th Earl checked his books and discovered that in one year alone Croome Court had consumed 290 tons of more expensive coal – and, in part, to ensure that everyone who lived in the great house, whether servant or master, would have access to hot water.

But the generosity and forward planning which characterised the 9th Earl's life were under threat. Although the parade of lavish house parties continued, and although the traditions of helping the tenants with handouts carried on, by the end of the Great War cracks had begun to appear in the life of the Coventry family and the estate itself had begun to struggle for survival. It seems to me, when I look back, that bad luck – or was it bad behaviour? – always seemed to dog the Coventrys. Just as the 9th Earl's predecessors had as often as not been wastrels and attracted scandal and public opprobrium in generous measure, his eldest son was to continue the tradition.

George William, Viscount Deerhurst, had been born in 1865. After the traditional aristocratic schooling at Eton, he went up to Cambridge. But the academic life bored him and he devoted his time at university to gambling and shooting. For the next few years he led a dissolute life and only an appointment as Aide de Camp to the Governor of Victoria in Australia avoided unpleasantness with a notorious bookmaker. But even on the other side of the world he couldn't live up to expectations of respectability and he got himself caught up in the great Australian Gold Rush, until he caught a dangerous fever and had to return home to England. A brief and unsuccessful career as a stockbroker on the London Exchange was followed by a new outbreak of gold-rush fever, this time in South

Africa. Armed with a rifle (for hunting game) and a shovel (for prospecting), he swaggered his way across the Cape until his deeply unimpressed father summoned him home again to Croome.

The country life obviously bored him though and he was soon back in London and back to his wastrel ways. He ran up huge gambling debts – owing the then vast sum of £17,000 (the equivalent of more than £3 million today) to a moneylender. In 1890 Lord Deerhurst was declared bankrupt. Somewhat reluctantly, the 9th Earl came to his financial aid but within a year scandal would once again come to haunt the Coventry name.

It all began with a game of cards. On 8 September 1890 the 9th Earl and the Countess of Coventry were attending a house party at the home of a wealthy shipping magnate near Hull. It was quite normal for the gentry to travel hundreds of miles to spend weekends at other rich folk's houses and, on this occasion – as often happened – they were joined by royalty: the Prince of Wales – the future Edward VI – was one of the assembled guests and after dinner all the gentlemen retired to the smoking room for a game of Baccarat. One of the players accused another – a colonel in the army – of cheating and, in the way of things back then, the alleged cheat was made to sign a secret undertaking, drawn up by Lord Coventry, that he would never play cards ever again.

That should have been the end of the matter but the story

leaked out to the newspapers – probably because the Prince of Wales was involved – and the colonel was dismissed from the army. Facing financial and social ruin, he sued all the gentlemen present – including the Prince and the Earl of Coventry – for libel. The case ended up in the High Court in London, with both Edward and Lord Coventry forced to give evidence on oath. Today, perhaps, such a case would attract little attention and no real damage would be done. But back then it caused a storm of scandal and, following on from Lord Deerhurst's very public bankruptcy, once again dragged the Coventry name through the mud.

Nor were relations inside the family any better. One of the great rooms at Croome Court – one that I would come to know well and where the future Countess of Coventry would teach me a new skill – was the Tapestry Room. Its walls were hung with the most gorgeous huge cloths of green damask, and the matching sofa and chairs were worth a small fortune. As the cost of maintaining Croome Court and the Estate grew and grew – annual expenditure on drainage for the parkland topped £1,000 (a whopping £200,000 today) - the Earl decided he had to part with some of its assets: the contents of the Tapestry Room were catalogued and sold off to a French collector for £50,000 – a handy £10 million today.

But the Earl's son was furious. The dissolute Lord Deerhurst was outraged that what he regarded as part of his inheritance should be so snatched away from him. After lengthy and acrimonious negotiations – which would drag on until 1920 – Deerhurst was allocated £5,000 from the money, with the balance to be invested for the benefit of the Coventry family (in other words, for him). All of this was once again played out, ignominiously, in public.

I sometimes wonder if my parents ever saw the reports of these scandals. Dad was a traditional working man – not particularly political, but Labour if anything – and he read the traditional working-man's newspaper, the *Daily Mirror*. It must have covered the various unfolding embarrassments but I don't recall anyone ever talking about them in our little home. Then again, times were different back then: somehow, the rules were different for rich and poor. We may have had little money but we were – and were expected to be – respectable. No dissolute lifestyle (I doubt we would have recognised the word!) for us: we never gambled anything more than a penny – at most – on a whist drive at the British Legion. And we'd been brought up in that solid, respectable belief that drink was a mocker of fools and led to bad ways. But the aristocracy? Well, it was different for them: somehow the sort of idle, even debauched, life they led was tolerated – was even expected. After all, they were the gentry. All in all, if Dad ever read about the scandals, he either dismissed them or didn't associate them with the family I was about to join and the life I was about to live.

Chapter Three

Apprenticeship

They called them The Hungry Thirties. A decade of financial crises, ever-rising unemployment, confusion, anger, a growing distrust of politicians and, as the years wore on, the looming shadow of another world war. 'Locust years', 'a dark tunnel', 'the Devil's Decade' – those were some of the phrases used back then. And time has done nothing to change the image of the 1930s. And always, always, throughout the length and breadth of the land, there was hunger.

We need, I think, to stop for a moment and talk about money because money was, of course, very different then to what it is now: not just in what it could buy (if you had it) but the actual money – coins and notes – was a whole different system to the one which almost all of you will have grown up with. I suppose I'm one of the few people still alive who can remember all the various coins we used then. So before their names – still romantic sounding to me – slip from the grasp of memory, I should tell you what was what.

Of course, the pound was still the basic unit of currency. But in those pre-decimal days there weren't 100 pennies in a pound: there were 12 pennies in a shilling and 20 shillings in a pound, which meant that a pound was made up of 240 pennies. I suppose that must sound terribly complicated to a generation – possibly two or three – brought up on the simplicity of our current coinage but, to us, it was as natural as the air we breathed. And at school when we learned our times table – always chanting it together until we knew it off by heart – we went up to 12 times 12 as a matter of routine. These days, when I fish in my purse for a coin and pull out a penny, it seems terribly small and insignificant because, back when I was growing up, a penny was a big, heavy round coin – it felt solid and reassuring in your pocket – nearly an inch and a half (I suppose you would say 30 millimetres) and made of good English brass.

The halfpenny was, as its name suggests, worth half of one penny but we also had farthings. There were four farthings in a penny and, for a child, a farthing was a very valuable commodity: one could buy you two big gobstoppers, a sweet guaranteed to keep you occupied for up to half an hour (if you were careful how you sucked it), or perhaps a lovely, chewy piece of liquorice. And if you happened to have four farthings – a whole penny – why, then you had a whole afternoon's confectionary delight to look forward to! As a child, a penny was a real treasure – and, like most families of our class, the pennies were counted and saved and looked after very, very carefully. Above a penny was a thruppeny bit: a solid-brass, 12-sided coin (though there were also some older silver thruppeny coins), worth three whole pennies, but which always seemed like the ugly duckling of our coinage. Sixpences were silver and everyone new them as a 'tanner'. A shilling was a 'bob', a two-shilling coin a florin (or, to us, a 'two-bob bit'). We even had another coin worth two shillings and sixpence called 'half a crown'.

Our notes, too, were different. Today we hand over five-pound notes without thinking much: they're almost a basic place to start and people are beginning to talk about phasing out the pound coin. That would have been unthinkable to us back then – not that we had pound coins. Paper money started with the ten-shilling note – with lovely brown-coloured engraving on it. Pound notes were green and, at least until the middle of the decade, five-pound notes were big white sheets of what felt like parchment. Not that we ever saw many five-pound (or even one-pound) notes: those were something from storybooks and comics, used by rich people, not ordinary folk living in little terraced cottages.

As this chapter goes on, we'll be talking about money quite a bit, so I need to explain the way money was written down. One penny was 1d; one shilling was 1s – so when you see figures like £1 17s 6d you will (I hope) know what I'm talking about.

It's easy for me to sit back and tell you that money was worth a lot more in those days: certainly a shilling – never mind a whole pound – would be enough to buy a bar of soap or a small loaf of bread, or a even cinema ticket. But clever people have worked out a way of translating the real value of a pound or a shilling in the 1930s compared to what it would buy today. There are, in fact, a whole set of different answers, depending on what is used as the yardstick but, for the purposes of this book, I've gone with the one that compares average weekly wages now and back then – although, as we'll see, that wasn't the whole story, not by a long chalk. Today the average wage before tax for a working man or woman is £442 per week; at the start of the 1930s it was between £3 and £4 – so you can see that we have to multiply the figures by at least 110 to get some idea of what they meant to ordinary families. In those days wages were paid – at least to the vast number of ordinary folk – in cash, in a little brown envelope at the end of every week. Most people didn't have bank accounts (although they might have had a savings book at the post office): bank accounts were for what we would today call white-collar workers – although back then they were known as black-coat employees, on account of the smart black jackets they would have to wear.

When the weekly wage came into the home, it was routinely handed over by the man of the house to his wife (although, for the less respectable families – and respectability was the big class divide in working families – some of it might have gone missing in the pub by the time the man rolled home on a Friday night). For good, honest, decent families (as we thought of ourselves), the woman would open the envelope and often divide up the wages into separate tins – one each for rent, food, gas, coal and so on: all the bills that would have to be paid – again in cash – mostly on a weekly basis. One of a wife's jobs was to run the weekly housekeeping budget, often scrimping and saving on one or other of the tins to ensure that the most pressing bills would be paid on time.

There were no credit cards, of course, but many families existed on 'tick' – credit at the local shop, or purchases of clothing from catalogue firms on the basis of a few pennies, or a shilling, a week. 'Neither a lender nor a borrower be' was, in respectable homes, something of a watch word.

For many households – and mine was one of them – there was a strict separation of duties between man and wife. It was the man's role to go out to work and bring home enough to support the whole family. A woman's work was largely in the home – and what work it was. The fire grate or the oven might be black-leaded every week, to keep it immaculate and respectably shiny. The front step had to be scrubbed with a brush and a bar of soap – if your front step wasn't spotless, neighbours would know that the family living inside was on the slide. The weekly washing was a laborious and time-consuming chore, with a peggy stick to stir the clothes in a big bucket of soapy water and a wooden washboard to scrub them. There was no electricity, so ironing had to be done with a heavy piece of cast iron heated up on the coal fire. Baking day was generally a Wednesday – again using a big old coal- or gas-fired stove. I don't know anyone today who regularly bakes their own bread – everyone seems to go to the supermarket and buy it pre-sliced as well as ready-made – but back then most wives and mothers would never dream of buying a loaf: not only was it an expensive luxury – and believe me we didn't have the money for those – but it was just another of the things expected of the woman of the house.

Children were expected to help too. All of us in the Mulley household went to the local school in Stamford but we were expected to help with the bed-making and the cleaning and generally make Mum's life a little easier.

Around 6pm was the woman's one bit of rest in those days. Often as not – and even in respectable families like ours – the man might go to the pub for a half pint of mild (bitter was more expensive and a whole pint meant a celebration) and his wife might get to put her feet up after a day's hard labour in the house.

That was how working-class life had always been: generation after generation knew its place and knew its duties and where in the fabric of family life the men and the women fitted in. But by the start of the 1930s something had come along to change this traditional balance – in fact, to knock it out of kilter forever more. Unemployment.

People today talk about unemployment and the state of the economy – and rightly so. But the 1930s were much more terrible than what Britain has been going through in the past few years. I was 13 and still at school when the decade began and I saw for myself how bad things were for ordinary people. When you see films or television programmes today set in the 1920s, they tend – like *Upstairs Downstairs* and *Downton Abbey* – to show life from the point of view of the rich and privileged. So we get the impression of that decade as one of glitz and excitement – the jazz age with its flappers and fancy frocks. But the financial troubles, which would make the

1930s a time of fear – terror even – in which people literally didn't have enough money to feed themselves, let alone keep a roof over their heads, began in that so-called decade of glamour.

The 1929 American stock-market crash set off global economic shockwaves. British exports, already falling in the 1920s, fell by half again and, as a result, people were put out of work on a mass scale. Unemployment rose to 3 million and, for them, the prospect was truly bleak. You see, we didn't have then the welfare state to catch and support people who lost their jobs.

There was a basic system of what was called unemployment insurance – when you had a job, you paid in a few shillings a week so that, if – or when – you got turfed out, you got something to keep you and your family going. But even that was pitifully small – no more than £1 17s – and, as the crisis worsened and the government got less and less money coming into the scheme, these already pitiful benefits were cut by ten per cent. Does that sound a lot? It should do because people were already struggling to pay their rent – which could often be as much as 40% of their regular income, never mind what they got when they lost their jobs – let alone buy food or put money aside for the gas bill. An official report of the time said that a man with a wife and two children needed to spend 19s and 9d each and every week just to buy enough food to stop them starving. That would leave just 17s and 3d to pay the rent – at least 15s a week – and all the other bare necessities of life.

What made it all even worse was that, as more and more people were laid off, a strict and cruel means test was introduced. In order to qualify for welfare handouts, an unemployed worker had to apply to the local Public Assistance Committee. These were just one step up from the old Victorian Poor Law relief – the system that resulted in desperate men, women and children being put into workhouses. And it was really only a very small step: the Committees – made up of the great and good – put the worker's finances through a rigorous investigation before they could qualify for benefit. Officials went into every detail of a family's income and savings. Sometimes they even took into account what furniture was in a home and insisted this be sold off. The mean-spirited intrusiveness of the means test and the insensitive manner of officials who carried it out was a terrible blight on people's lives. Many people began slowly to starve.

My Dad had experienced the first taste of what was to come when, after the First World War, he couldn't get his old job at the engineering works back. He did, as we've seen, what many other men with pride and integrity and nowhere else to turn did, setting himself up as a boot and shoe repairer. Now this wasn't a proper business at all. He didn't have a shop or premises where customers could come: his workshop was our back yard or, occasionally, the front room. But in this way he somehow managed to keep us afloat – often with my aunt at the hotel slipping us items of leftover food. I don't to this day know how he did it but he took pride in being resourceful, and he insisted on a smart turnout – no backsliding for Dad – with his shoes polished to a gleaming shine every morning. He even managed to find enough money for a few cigarettes – but in those days these were cheap: Woodbines – always the working-man's smoke – were 2d for five.

Not everyone was able to manage like we did and, as the numbers of men unemployed rose and rose, many went 'on the tramp': trudging many miles each day from town to town in the hope of finding any sort of paid work. But even this was often hopeless and it wasn't long before other marches began to happen. Hunger marches, they called them: hundreds of unemployed men from all over the country determinedly setting out in an organised group to march on London in the hope of persuading the government to take notice of their plight. More than one of them – for there were many – came through Stamford. They processed – a long, disciplined snake of men with hollow faces and some carrying banners – through the main street. At lunchtime they stopped outside the Crown Hotel and somehow food was found for them, given free in acknowledgement, I suppose, that there but for the grace of God could be our own menfolk.

Still, we were the lucky ones in all this. While unemployment rose to 2.5 million and, in some areas, the proportion out of work reached 70 per cent, and quarter of the population existed on a subsistence diet, often with signs of child malnutrition such as scurvy, rickets and tuberculosis, I was growing up in the heart of a warm, loving family. And, between them, Mum and Dad managed to insulate their three young children from the worst of the hard times.

Money was, of course, very scarce so, when we weren't at school or helping around the house, we tended to make use of such free entertainment as we could. I had always loved swimming and in those days it was perfectly normal for children to be allowed to go out and play in the river. The River Welland begins more than a hundred miles away in Northamptonshire and flows sluggishly north-eastwards to The Wash on the edge of East Anglia. The Romans had used it to transport food between their settlements and it has been part Stamford's character ever since. Growing up, Mum and Dad would send us off – sometimes with a sandwich packed in greaseproof paper – to swim in one of the shallower parts of its course. I loved it: feeling the cool, fresh water on my skin was so much better than a trip to the Municipal Baths and in those days

Stamford felt as safe as safe can be for a youngster. What was more, it was completely free!

But one day all this changed. It wasn't a day that I went swimming but we heard about it soon enough. Edith, a school friend of mine, just about the same age as me, had somehow got out of her depth or caught her foot in the reeds and drowned. There – in our safe, lovely old river. Well, that was enough for Dad: he put his foot down straight away and told all of us that we'd made our last trip to the Welland. Looking back, I can, of course, see his point – although it was rare for Dad to be so stern with us. Mum was the one who wore the trousers in our house and everything had to be done exactly as she wanted. Even to this day, when I have carers coming in to help me, I still remake the bed after they've gone because it wouldn't live up to Mum's exacting standards. Dad, though, was a softie – a gentle, kind man who rarely, if ever, raised his voice: perhaps that's what made his instruction that the river was now out of bounds all the more forceful. But at the time I think I must have felt a confusing mixture of sorrow at my friend's death, fear for what we had all escaped and sadness that we'd no longer be able to enjoy one of our few, cost-free pleasures. My sister Joan and I carried on swimming every day but we had to go to the freezing-cold outdoor Municipal Pool from that moment on.

By this time I was 14 and I knew that my schooldays

were coming to an end. In those days children – at least children from ordinary families – went to primary school until the age of 13, then on to what we could call a secondary school today for just 12 months. It wasn't until 1936 – by which time I was 20 – that the school-leaving age was raised to 15.

I'd been at All Saints Elementary School, studying what we then called the Three Rs: reading, writing and arithmetic (I never understood why a word beginning with A was counted as an R!) until it was time to take exams. If you passed them, you went to the Grammar – or High – School; if you didn't you went to one that was less academic and more attuned to teaching vocational skills like woodwork, cookery and suchlike. Well, I was lucky: I passed my exams – I'd always loved and had an aptitude for maths, and reading was a pleasure – so off I went to big school.

The first thing you – or your children – would notice if I could whisk you back in time would be how strict everything was at school. There was no chattering in the classroom and teachers had to be treated with respect. Honestly, I look at what I see on television these days and wonder if today's children would last five minutes in the school I went to: not one of the teachers would take the sort of cheek that seems to happen every day in modern classes and, if anyone did dare to stray out of line … well, the cane was there and was used in double-quick time. Spare the rod and spoil the child was the policy in those days – and there wasn't much in the way of spoiling going on, I can tell you.

All the girls – it was, of course, a girls-only school; no one ever thought that boys and girls should mix in those days – had to wear a uniform. There was a gymslip – the sort you see in the *St. Trinians* films – over a white blouse. Both of these had to be kept ironed nice and crisp. And the school tie had to be knotted neatly beneath the collar: none of the slovenly half-mast arrangements kids get away with today (even if they actually have to wear a tie). No – the motto was smartness and that extended down to our knickers: rough green serge was the order of the day.

We also had to wear sensible shoes and, even if the school hadn't insisted, Dad would have made sure that we were properly shod. It was one of his most important personal rules: always have good strong, sensible shoes, and I'm very thankful to him for it. At my age – and much younger – lots of people suffer with their feet and it's because they were allowed to wear silly fashion shoes that pinched or distorted their feet. And, as luck would have it, when I did disregard Dad's advice, it was shoes that got me into trouble – but we're not at that point in our story yet.

School strictness also extended to timekeeping. Not one of us had a wristwatch – we'd never have thought of anything like that, even if we'd been able to afford it – but the school was very strict about arriving on time and not being late for classes. I often wonder where that has gone: people today – and I don't just mean youngsters – seem to regard time as something completely flexible. And yet everyone today has a watch and a phone that tells them where they're due and when: yet everyone is always late.

It's an old saying that schooldays are the best days of your life: that's another thing that has changed in this modern world – I can't imagine today's children thinking like that, not one bit. And I'm happy to say that I loved school – stern though the teachers were and highly-disciplined though the lessons were. I suppose, now I come to think of it, that in this way school was an extension of the way parents like mine brought up their children: work hard, respect your elders, speak when you're spoken to and stick by the rules. The funny thing is that I would only learn later how these simple rules for life didn't seem to apply to our so-called betters. But I'm getting ahead of myself again …

So there I was, Hilda Mary Mulley, aged 15: what was I going to do with my life? There were five of us in the little terraced cottage and it was obvious that with money so tight I'd have to start earning my keep. But what to do?

In a way, I suppose it was almost pre-ordained. My grandfather – Mum's dad – had been a professional tailor and, as a child, I would often stand and watch him as he cut the cloth and, as I grew older, I used to help him take all the tacks out of whatever he was making for his clients. And at school I'd always been good at needlework – enjoyed it too. So, with Mum and Dad's help, I set about trying to find an apprenticeship as a dressmaker.

Stamford, like most towns in those days, had at least one tailoring business. People frequently had their clothes made for them – ordinary clothes for everyday wear, not fancy ones for big occasions. It wasn't like today's world where everyone seems to go shopping for off-the-peg jackets, trousers or dresses. And we wouldn't have ever heard the word 'designer', much less look at a label to see if a garment had been made by some fashionable name.

Mrs Kent ran one of these little operations. She didn't have a shop, with clothes in the window. Instead – much like my Dad, I suppose – she had a workshop but she employed about ten people, making ordinary clothes for ordinary people and, as luck would have it, she wanted an apprentice. Now, I know that apprenticeships have rather gone out of fashion (more's the pity), so I'd better tell you how it worked back in 1931 when I started my adult life.

An apprenticeship was a long, drawn-out business: two years as a full apprentice, followed by two more as an indentured worker – that meant you weren't allowed to leave, even if you got a better offer. The second thing, which was very much an indicator of the terrible economic times we were living in, was that apprenticeships didn't come for free. To get me taken on by Mrs Kent meant that Mum had to pay her a £25 registration fee: 25 whole pounds – at least £2,500 in today's money – and more than 20 times what people got in their weekly unemployment benefit. Where, or how, she found the money I'll never know: I don't even know whether it was a deposit that she got back at the end of my four years – although I rather doubt it. But find it she did and at the age of 15 I was an apprentice dressmaker.

I wonder what people in my position would be paid today. There is, of course, the minimum wage now – something we could never have dreamed of in those dark days of the 1930s. Well, I can tell you what my weekly pay was: one shilling a week. Think about that for a moment and compare it to what your earned in your first job, or what your children earn today. One shilling – 12 old pennies. Not enough to buy a whole loaf of bread. And from this shilling I had to pay Mum for my bed and board at home: I was an adult now and I had to pay my way. I tell you what that did: it taught me to value money and, if I wasted it – on a trip to the cinema or a penny bun on the way back from the swimming pool – why, then I wasted it wisely!

I was the lowest of the low in the little workshop. As an

apprentice, I started out by picking up pins from the floor – pins the older and more experienced girls had dropped – and taking the tacks out of half-made clothes. That's how I learned my trade – watching and picking up and unpicking. I certainly wasn't allowed near a pair of scissors (much less a piece of valuable cloth) until at least a year had passed. But I loved the work: I loved the whole feeling of being around a process that created clothes for people to wear. And who knows but I might catch sight of the very garment I'd had a hand in, walking around Stamford. It made me proud.

Gradually, as I progressed in my apprenticeship, the other girls would allow me to take the dress or the trousers they'd been working on away and I'd be shown how to press open the seams they'd created with a big heavy steam iron. And from there to the day – the exciting, scary day – when I was given my first piece of material and my first pattern and told to cut the cloth for myself. Now that was a special day, I can tell you.

Until one day I was no longer an apprentice, no longer even an indentured employee. Somehow, four years had passed: I was 19 and a fully-trained tailor, and the world, if not at my feet, was very definitely laid out in front of me on the dress-making table. And then Mrs Kent upped and died. I was out of a job.

At that time, when you finished an apprenticeship, you

had to apply to be taken on again as a full employee. With Mrs Kent gone, there was no one to hire me, so I had to start looking elsewhere. But this was The Hungry Thirties: there were no jobs for a newly qualified tailor – in fact, there were precious few jobs at all. In the end, I was offered a position in the laundry room at the George Hotel – Stamford's other residential inn. It was my job to dish out the sheets and keep everything ship-shape and tidy. And I hated it. I felt it was below me: mind-numbing work and tiring to boot. Nor was it very well paid and, even if I'd thought of it, there was no chance of supplementing my meagre wages with a little work behind the bar. Dad wouldn't have stood for that: pulling pints and serving drinks wasn't what we called respectable.

I must have been at the George for several months when one of the other girls who worked there asked why I didn't think about going into service. I remember to this day her coming to me and saying, 'I'm surprised you're doing this job, what with all your training. Why don't you apply for a job as a Lady's maid?' And in that moment my future was sealed.

Chapter Four

An Idea from a Work Colleague

The Honourable Nesta Donne Phillips was born into a life of privilege and luxury on 20 November 1903. She was the eldest of three daughters born to Owen Cosby Phillips, first and last Baron Kylsant, Member of Parliament, High Sheriff of Pembrokeshire and chairman of one of the country's greatest steamship companies.

Mr Phillips, as he had once been, was the son of a parson who, at a young age, had been apprenticed to a shipping firm in Newcastle-Upon-Tyne – then the beating heart of the Empire's all-powerful fleet. He worked his way up through the company and, by degrees, through other shipping businesses until, in 1902, he became managing director of the Royal Mail Steam Packet Company. Within 20 years this had bought out the famous White Star Line

– the company that owned and was responsible for the ill-fated *Titanic* – for the tidy sum of £7 million (£700 million today) to become the largest shipping group in the world. He was invested as a Knight Grand Cross, Order of St Michael and St George (G.C.M.G.) and in 1923 was created 1st Baron Kylsant of Carmarthen and of Amroth, in the County of Pembroke. The family seat was Amroth Castle, a grand 18th-century house, built on the remains of Norman ruins, with expansive grounds stretching down to the beautiful Pembrokeshire coast.

His eldest daughter grew up surrounded by wealth and eligible young men, and the man she chose to be her husband was the Honourable George William Coventry, the grandson of the 9th Earl. By the time of the wedding, a lavish affair in Carmarthen in September 1921, the Earl of Coventry was 83 years old but still hale and hearty and in residence at Croome Court. Since his son was the next in line and, therefore, would inherit the title and all that went with it, George William can't have had any expectation of coming into his own inheritance for decades to come. But within a decade a series of family catastrophes would change everything.

The troubles started in 1926 and it was the Great Depression that began them. Lord Kylsant was facing increasing difficulties in repaying government loans to his shipping empire: he had been expecting an improvement in world trade following the First World War but, after a decade of peace, this had not materialised. Increased competition from foreign companies was making life very difficult for his businesses. Despite this, Kylsant bought two more companies, apparently taking an unrealistically rosy view of the future. As trade slumped, his economic woes mounted.

A year later the Coventry family was hit by what newspapers termed 'The Curse of The Deerhursts': the 9th Earl's son and heir – George William Coventry's father – died unexpectedly. It was the second time in living memory that the sitting Earl had outlived his son. George William and his young wife Nesta now knew that before long they would have to take on the title and, with it, the escalating costs of Croome Court.

It can't have been easy: although gentry such as the Coventrys seemed to have much more wealth and many more resources to fall back on than ordinary folk, they also faced huge inheritance-tax bills on top of the constant haemorrhaging of money at Croome. And, for Nesta, financial troubles at home were looming ever larger.

In 1929 the Bank of England was so concerned about the solvency of Lord Kylsant's combined shipping companies that it sent one of the most famous accountants in the country in to examine all the business records. Within two months he discovered that the group had liabilities of more than £30 million – that's £3 billion today.

As the crisis mounted throughout 1930 and 1931, speculation grew in the press about Lord Kylsant's future. Despite this, he and Lady Kylsant left England at the start of February for a two-month holiday in South Africa. But almost as soon as they returned, Lord Kylsant was arrested and charged with criminal offences of fraud. The case was transferred to the Central Criminal Court – known to you and me as the Old Bailey – and after a 9-day trial Kylsant was convicted and sentenced to 12 months in prison. It must have been a nightmarish time for Nesta, not only to see her family fortunes evaporate but to watch as her father was led away to spend the next year as a common criminal in Wormwood Scrubs. There could be no greater disgrace.

But if things were bad for Nesta, her husband had also suffered a double tragedy. On 13 March 1930, following an illness that lasted 12 days, the 9th Earl of Coventry passed away, aged nearly 92. His death – which, as we saw, was reported in newspapers and in cinema newsreels – had a fatal effect on his wife. The couple had been married for 65 years and Lady Blanche told her grandson that she could not bear to be without the man she loved. The Countess of Coventry immediately took to her bed. Within three days she, too, was dead. A joint funeral was arranged and tenants from Croome and the surrounding villages crammed into the family church on the estate and lined the way for the cortège.

And that is how George William became the 10th Earl of Coventry and his wife, Nesta Donne, became the Countess. Within a few short years I would become her closest and most intimate servant, and Croome Court would become my home.

At the time, of course, I was still living with Mum and Dad in our little house in Vine Street in Stamford and still – albeit unhappily – working in the linen room at the Crown Hotel. But the idea of becoming a lady's maid had been planted in my mind by one of the other girls on the hotel staff.

The question was, though, how to go about it? How did an ordinary girl like me find out about possible openings with the gentry? I was sure I would be up to the job – if only I could find a way in! The first thing to do was to talk to my Aunt Beat: not only was she my godmother but she had once been in service herself. We were a close family and, particularly during the years that Dad had been away at the Western Front, my aunts had helped Mum greatly, so that she had come to trust their advice.

When I sat down with Aunt Beat, she was enthusiastic about my idea: she could see a whole different world opening up for me, a world away from little old Stamford and, I think, a route into a settled and comfortable life, which would be less prone to the buffeting of the economic ill winds that were sweeping the country. But when we talked to Dad, he was vehemently against it: he was very far from convinced about service as a suitable life for his daughter and was very worried about the prospect of me leaving home. Maybe that sounds a little strange to modern ears. After all, I was 19 and today no one thinks twice about young people of that age setting out to forge their own future. But in 1935, not only was 19 two years under the legal age at which a child became an adult but I think we all grew up much more slowly: a 19-year-old girl like me was, back then, nowhere near as worldly wise as someone of a similar age today. Of course, we were much less exposed to the world then: there was no television, no Internet – no one we knew even had a telephone. The upside of this was that families were much, much closer: the downside is that – for girls in particular – parents were very much more protective.

I'd had first-hand experience of this. As the eldest, I was the first to start going out of an evening. In addition to trips to the cinema, I loved dancing. The Assembly Rooms in Stamford put on dances every week – proper dances with a proper orchestra of ten or more musicians. They would play all the popular dances of the 1920s and 1930s – the Charleston, the Foxtrot and, if it was a particularly racy orchestra, daring crazes like the Tango and the Black Bottom.

My favourite was always the Waltz – a much more serene affair and suitably seemly for Dad's daughter. I had started to go to the Assembly Rooms when I was 15, handing over a hard-won thruppeny bit for the entrance fee. There was, of course, no question of alcohol being served: it was squash or a cup of tea – not even so much as a hint of beer. At first, Mum or Aunt Beat would take me – both of them loved dancing – but when I turned 16, I was allowed to go on my own. Dad took a very close interest in what I got up to: he insisted on walking me there the first few times, just to see what this dance business was all about and, even when he let me go there unaccompanied, he would always be waiting up for me when it was home time. I used to walk back down the street and, whatever the time, would see a light on in Mum and Dad's bedroom: I knew he would be waiting at the window, peering out to check up on who had walked me home.

That was a big thing back then: boys who liked the look of you would, after a couple of dances, be asking who was walking you home – it was quite unthinkable that a young lady should walk herself home alone! This was one of the first stages in courtship in those days and, if this developed, your friends and family would know you were 'walking out' with so-and-so. How innocent this all seems in today's liberated world: there was no question back then of any hanky panky – a kiss on the cheek might be considered very daring!

It's not for me to say this but I had a decent figure and a nice little waist and I suppose I must have been pretty enough to attract the attention of some of the local boys: they certainly asked if they could walk me home! I like to think that at least some of it was down to my skill as a tailor, for I made my own dresses to go dancing and one in particular – a lovely pale-blue satin material, which Mum had bought for me at Stamford Market, and which (thanks to my apprenticeship with Mrs Kent) looked like something from a very fancy couturier – drew attention the moment I walked into the Assembly Rooms wearing it. The girls all flocked round me with little cries of, 'Molly,' (I was always known as Molly in those days), 'Did you really make that? It's so lovely!' I think the boys noticed it too – I certainly saw them sneaking glances my way – but I already had a young man I was walking out with. Norman Aitkin was his name and he worked at Blackstone's, the engineering company in the town, which had once employed Dad. I thought he was smashing. But Dad – oh, dear, Dad – he just didn't approve at all. Whether he would have thought anyone good enough for his eldest daughter is debatable. Maybe it was because Dad couldn't get his old job back at Blackstone's after the war, maybe it was the fact that he didn't like Norman's mother but, for whatever reason, in his eyes, Norman Aitkin was definitely not up to snuff.

Although I'd been allowed to go to dances on my own for some months by the time Norman and I started courting, once Dad knew we were walking out, there was nothing for it but that I had to have a chaperone. If Norman and I went anywhere together, my little brother Jim was sent out to find us and make sure Norman behaved himself on the way home.

So, all in all, Dad was never going to welcome the idea of his darling daughter leaving home and going into service miles away. Don't forget that, once I'd gone, he knew there would be little or no chance of coming to see me: we didn't have a car – no one from our class of people could even dream of running one, let alone paying the £175 even a basic one would cost. (If that sounds terribly little money for a car, don't forget to multiply it by 100 to work out the modern equivalent: could you afford to splash out £17,500 if you were in our position today? Of course, car prices have come down in relative terms since then but in 1935 motoring was still very much in its infancy and the purchase price of even a little Austin or a Morris reflected that.) Nor were there any buses in Stamford: if you wanted to get anywhere locally, well, it was 'Shanks's pony' as everyone called walking. There was, though, the train station and I began to wonder whether one of the enormous puffing steam engines that pulled in amid a fearsome clanking of steel and vast clouds of smoke might one day take me away from the town in which I had lived all my life.

In the end it was the girl at work – the same one who had put the idea of my going into service in the first place – who helped me make a start. To this day I don't know how she found out about the opportunities: maybe she had seen an advert from one of the agencies which then advertised positions in service for girls like me. But however she knew, I was at work in the laundry room one day when she came to me with the news that two fine ladies were looking for a maid. And she challenged me to write to them.

The first was Lady Blanche Cobbold, from Glemham Hall near Ipswich in Suffolk. Since this was close to where Dad had grown up before he made the journey to Stamford, perhaps he would look on the idea more favourably. Lady Cobbold was, in fact, the daughter of the ninth Duke of Cavendish, and one of the most illustrious women in the country. She had been born and raised at the family estate at Chatsworth; she was married to a brave and dashing soldier who had been wounded in the Great War and had two young daughters. It certainly seemed like a very promising opening.

The other was Nesta, Countess of Coventry. I knew nothing about her at the time and Worcestershire, where she lived at Croome Court, seemed an awful long way away. Nonetheless, I resolved to write to both the Countess and Lady Cobbold, enquiring about a position as their lady's maid.

I don't know what I would have done if both had replied – quite probably, I would have preferred to go to Suffolk, given Dad's connection with the county. But as it happened it was Lady Coventry who sent me a handwritten note inviting me to come for an interview.

First, though, there was the little question of getting Dad's permission. He was quite adamantly opposed to the whole scheme and, since it was so rare for Dad really to put his foot down, I knew that I would need allies. Fortunately, Mum and my aunts were both on my side: together we slowly won Dad over and I was granted his blessing to go for the interview.

The funny thing is that, however much I try, I can't remember a thing about it. You might put that down to my age but I'm convinced it was nerves: I'd never been outside of Stamford and my interview was in Worcester – miles and miles away and, as far as I was concerned, a big city. I couldn't tell you how I got there, nor what was said by the Countess – much less what I said to her. But somehow or other I must have done well enough, for a few days later a letter arrived at Vine Street, addressed to me in a firm handwriting style: her Ladyship was pleased to accept me for the position of her lady's maid.

Well, what an excitement there was in our little house. Everything that I owned – not that there was much – needed to be packed up into a little cardboard suitcase. I would need suitable clothes (out came the sewing machine) and strong sensible shoes. Even though it was summertime, because I was going to a grand mansion, I would also need a hat – women and men always wore hats to go anywhere in those days – and gloves. I'd also needed the fare for my journey, which wasn't to be sneezed at in our frugal household. Above all, I'd have to find out how to get there. And this journey I do remember clearly

I don't know if you can imagine what it was like nearly 80 years ago for a young girl to set out on an adventure like this. These days, of course, it's easy to find train times and everyone is used to travelling all over the place. But in those days very few people ever strayed more than a mile or so from their hometown and the transport system was cumbersome and rather daunting – at least to a girl like me. After a trip to the station to consult the big and complicated book of railway timetables, we worked out that I would have to take three separate trains. The first would take me from Stamford to Leicester. Here I would get off and have to locate the train bound for

Birmingham. Once I got there, I had to change again, this time onto the local service for Worcester. All in all, what with the slowness of the steam engines and waiting on the platforms at each stage, the journey was going to take all day: and this for a journey of just over a hundred miles.

Slowly, the day for my departure came around. My suitcase was packed and I laid out a nice new dress, the thick black stockings everyone wore in those days, hat, gloves and – of course – my shoes polished to within an inch of their lives. My heart was racing as I closed the door on the little bedroom I shared with Joan: this was it – I was off out into the big wide world and who could know when, or if ever, I'd see my home and my family again?

Dad was very upset: I knew how much he was worried and how much he didn't want me to go. But, being Dad, he was strong and supportive and smiling: men didn't show their emotions much in those days and I don't think Dad would have ever dreamed of letting me, or even Mum, see the tears he must have been keeping in check. But as we walked through the town towards the station, I knew he was dreading the moment when I climbed aboard the train and he would watch as it pulled out, taking me away from my family.

At the small ticket window, the railway clerk took my money and punched out the little oblong piece of thick cardboard: my ticket to a new life. It was, of course, Third

Chapter Five

Hierarchies

'Miss Mulley, is it?'

The man in front of me was a few inches taller than me but his dark hair had been combed back from his forehead (into what looked very much like the sort of brush Mum had used to sweep up with), which made him seem taller. Hair or no hair, as I appraised him, I reckoned he was a few inches taller than me and about ten years older. He was wearing a smart dark suit, his shoes were nicely shined (always a good sign – Dad's training again) and a peaked cap. It didn't take a genius to work out that this must be the Coventry's chauffeur. I'm not sure what I expected, but fancy that: a real chauffeur meeting little Hilda Mary Mulley off the train – how very posh indeed!

I didn't have much time to take this in though: as the train pulled out, leaving clouds of smoke and steam rolling along the platform, the chauffeur was marching smartly off to the exit. 'Well,' I thought, 'Here goes. What's to be afraid of anyway?' I'm not sure if I answered my own question. If I had, I think I could have found plenty of reasons why my stomach was in knots and I felt a bit sick. I'd spent a day criss-crossing England, changing trains, drinking cups of tea poured from big silver urns in smoky station buffets, watching mile after mile of countryside sweep past the window – and now here I was, about to pledge the rest of my life (because that's how I thought of it) to the service of a rich and powerful Countess I'd barely met. I hadn't the first clue of where I was going and, if the chauffeur seemed perfectly at ease – and, therefore, I could presume he knew how we would get to our destination – why, I didn't even know his name. Nervous? Well, wouldn't you be?

Parked in the road outside the station was a very ordinary little blue van – the sort which butchers and similar tradesmen used back home in Stamford to make their rounds and deliveries. Surely this wasn't how we were to travel? But yes: the chauffeur was striding towards it, my little cardboard case in hand. What was his name? I couldn't really imagine driving to wherever we were going and calling him 'Mr Chauffeur'. What was the correct way of addressing him? These things would matter – that much I knew. I hurried to catch up.

The chauffeur held the door open for me and, as demurely as I could, I sat myself down in the old, worn seat. Instantly, I noticed a strange smell – what on earth could this be? Then with a bang and a slam the door was shut, the chauffeur swung himself into the driving seat and we were off.

'I'm Roland,' he said with a smile. 'Roland Newman. I'm Lord Coventry's driver. Amongst other things. Oh, please excuse the smell: this is the hound wagon.'

Hound wagon? Did the gentry's dogs have their very own car? I'd grown up with dogs – instantly I remembered our dear old mongrel at home in Vine Street – but we'd never had a car for ourselves, much less a separate one for the dog. What on earth sort of life had I come to?

Roland didn't seem to think anything of it though, so I sat quietly, pulling myself as tightly down into the seat as possible as the little van grumbled its way out of Worcester and on into the countryside. Miles and miles of it: fields ripe unto the harvest, as we used to sing at church back home. Corn, wheat and something else I didn't recognise at all.

'Those are hop fields,' Roland informed me. 'This part of Worcestershire is famous for its hops: we grow the best for the best beer in England.'

Since I'd never drunk beer – alcohol really wasn't part of Mulley family life – I had no answer to this. I tucked it away in the back of my mind: a new piece of information for my new life. This was certainly going to be an education.

The journey seemed to take forever – although I suppose it can't have been much more than an hour. We seemed to be going ever deeper into the countryside, with only the occasional small village giving any indication that people actually lived here. Just how remote was this place I was going to? And if it was so far away from any sort of civilisation – for that's how I thought of towns like Stamford – how would I ever to get away from it? That's what it began to feel like: that I would be a prisoner in some terribly isolated castle, with no hope of ever escaping. The further we went, the more nervous and uneasy I became.

Roland seemed unconcerned: if he noticed how worried I was becoming, he didn't show it. Instead, he kept up a cheerful (and largely one-sided) chatter about this and that. I couldn't tell you what he said, or whether he was trying to impart some knowledge that I would need in my new position: his words washed over my poor muddled head, filled with worries, until it blended in with the rattling of the little van's engine and the rumble of its wheels on the rough country roads.

And then, suddenly, there was the big stone gateway in

front of us. The soft, buttery afternoon light caught one side of it as the van pulled up.

'This is the London Arch,' Roland informed me as we passed beneath its huge weathered face. London? Surely we hadn't gone as far as that? London was a place I'd only ever read about in books and was as exotic and foreign sounding as Timbuktu. 'No, don't be silly,' I told myself. 'We can't have driven all the way to London.' Maybe this was one of the capital city's famous monuments and Lord Coventry had brought it all the way to Worcestershire. If so, he must be very rich indeed.

As these thoughts whirled through my head, the little van was off again, rumbling down a windy and very well-kept driveway. Trees – they seemed like a whole big wood to me – passed on my side while, on the other, open parkland spread out like an enormous bowling green for as far as I could see. Then we were onto crunching gravel and the car was stopping and Croome Court – bigger than any building I had ever seen in my young life – was in front of us. It was imposing, it was magnificent, it was impossibly grand: and, as Roland opened the car door and I slid out, my heart sank even lower. However beautiful, this place was like some giant prison castle in a storybook and I was to be locked up here with no hope of anyone coming to rescue me and no prospect of escape. If I hadn't been so terrified, I might have burst out crying there and then.

Roland picked up my case and walked me around the side of the house to the back. The rear of the house was just as impressive as the front: there was an enormous entrance with a pillared portico and huge stone steps leading up from the driveway. For a moment I wondered if I was going to have to march up those steps and in through the very grand doors. But Roland took me towards a little, almost hidden, entrance at the side.

'Tradesmen's entrance,' he said with a warm smile. Had he guessed what I'd been thinking? As he opened the door, I caught a glimpse of long half-lit passageways: we seemed to be heading into some strange subterranean world that echoed with the sound of our footsteps. I shuddered as we left the warm summer sunlight behind us and the cold basement air enveloped me.

On and on we walked through an endless series of corridors that seemed to sprout off one another and head off in all directions. How on earth would I ever find my way around this maze of passages? And did I really want to? The further we ventured into the depths of the house, the more I felt like an explorer entering some bottomless series of tunnels – and the more I wished I'd never left my cosy little home, with all its simplicity and its warmth, back in Stamford. 'Oh, you silly, silly girl,' I thought. 'What have you done?'

Eventually, we emerged from the latest of these passages

and into an enormous room. A huge cooking range ran down the side of one wall and people – other servants, I realised – bustled in and out. Occasionally, a bell would ring from somewhere in the maze of corridors and more bustling would happen. I had arrived at the beating heart of the house: the mighty kitchen of Croome Court.

Someone – I couldn't have told you who – pressed a cup of tea into my hands and a stern-looking older man appeared beside me. Of Roland the chauffeur there was now no sign. The new man welcomed me solemnly and explained that, given the lateness of the hour, I wouldn't be meeting my mistress tonight. Instead, I was to be shown to my bedroom, where I could make myself at home and prepare myself for work the next morning.

I had not the faintest idea what my duties would be, much less what time I would be expected to start performing them. But I was so tired, and felt so sorry for myself, that I simply followed a young woman in the uniform of what I assumed to be a maid out of the kitchen and back through the echoing passageways until we came to a great stone staircase, which seemed to rise and rise in front of my bewildered eyes. My guide tiptoed up the stairs to a little half-landing: this, she told me, was the floor where the Court's great reception rooms were. Then it was up to the next floor – the master and mistress's bedrooms, as well as those of the children, apparently – and up again until we reached the very top of the house. I'd never been up so many stairs in my life.

Off the top of the staircase was a little ante-room. At first, I thought this must be my bedroom: it was bigger than the room I shared with Joan back home but there was no sign of a bed. But we left this behind and the girl opened another door and then I simply gasped: the room in front of me was absolutely vast – I thought you could have plonked the whole of our house in Vine Street into this one room and still have had space left over. The ceiling was at least 15 feet above my head and there was the grandest fireplace I'd ever set eyes on in the middle of one wall. A little bed (though still bigger than my own at home) stood out against another wall, absolutely dwarfed by the open space around it. An enormous mahogany wardrobe loomed large in the corner. Surely all this couldn't be just for me?

But it was: if Croome Court was my prison, my 'cell' was, at least, incredibly spacious. I wandered over to the window – itself bigger than anything I'd ever been used to – and looked out: I saw lawns and a lazy river and, away in the distance, another remarkable building with huge glass windows on which the last of the day's light was reflected. I couldn't believe my eyes.

The girl was telling me something as she closed the door. I heard the words 'cup of tea' and 'bath' but really didn't register them. After she had left, I sat down on the bed, my little suitcase with all my worldly possessions neatly folded inside, looked around at all the empty splendour of my new surroundings … and burst into tears.

I cried myself to sleep that night – as I would do for weeks to come – thinking about the home I'd left behind me and the life I'd so carelessly abandoned. We might not have had much and Vine Street might have been a humble little place but, amid all the magnificence of Croome Court and its surrounding estate, I would have given absolutely anything to return to it.

I was woken the next morning by the same girl. She had a cup of tea in her hand and told me that my bath was ready. The tea I could understand but what was this about a bath? And who could have got it ready? Surely this couldn't be happening to me. Why would someone have run me a bath? And, anyway, where was it? I looked around, trying to see whether someone had deposited the sort of tin tub I was used to in one of the distant corners of the room. There was, of course, no sign of any such thing.

Instead, the girl – I still didn't know who, or what, she was – led me along yet another corridor and through a doorway into a room almost as big as my bedroom. In it was a large enamelled bath, brimming with hot, steaming water. It was a very long way from the Mulley household's

Friday ritual of a quick dip in the old tin tub in front of the fire. Was this a special occasion to mark my first day? Or was this to be a regular thing? No one had ever waited on me – surely that's what I was here to do? Either way, this little bit of my new life was a very pleasant surprise and perhaps I could grow to like at least this part of it.

I wondered, too, about when I would meet my new mistress. I hadn't seen her since that day in Worcester when I'd had my interview. I wanted to find out what my duties were and that would only happen when she told me. As it turned out, I didn't see her for the rest of the day. I spent the ensuing hours trying to find my way round the house – or, at least, the bits of it where I was supposed to go. I avoided the first and second floors: they were reserved for the Coventrys and, as I discovered, the staff only went there when they were called, or as part of their work when the family wasn't around.

First, I had to get to know about the other servants. I quickly found that there was a hierarchy below stairs: a very definite mini-social order, which I would be expected to understand and stick to. There were 15 of us in total who worked in the household, plus gardeners and a houndsman, who never ventured across the threshold. The lowliest of all was the scullery maid, a young girl just starting out in service who – whether because of her position or for family reasons – lived out in High Green, one of the little hamlets that surrounded the estate. Her job was, perhaps, the hardest and least rewarding of all: she acted as assistant to the kitchen maid, who was one rung above her on the social ladder, and there was a definite chain of command when it came to her duties. She reported to the kitchen maid, who, in turn, reported to the cook. Her orders would be passed down to her through each of these other two servants and, likewise, she passed messages back up the line via them. The poor scullery maid's duties included the most physical and demanding tasks in the kitchen, such as cleaning and scouring the old stone floor, which was so uneven that you swayed from foot to foot as you walked across it. She was also required to scrub the stove, the sinks, and all the pots and dishes. There was no washing-up liquid in those days: she had to scour all the crockery and cooking pans with soap crystals whisked up into a rough sort of lather.

On top of all this, she was expected to help with preparing the food for every meal – cleaning the vegetables, plucking fowl (which came in fresh with all their feathers, heads and claws on). If fish was on the menu, these would be delivered almost straight from the river and it was the scullery maid's task to gut and de-scale every one before the cook got her hands on them. Her day also began before anyone else's: while the rest of us still slumbered in our beds, the scullery maid started before

6am, getting the kitchen fire going and make sure the cooking range was lit ready for the day's cooking. Since she lived out, she had to walk a couple of miles to the Court from her home: woe betide her if she wasn't on time because all the other staff's jobs depended on her having got the kitchen and the fires ready for them when they came down. All in all, hers was a hard and backbreaking job and I was distinctly relieved I didn't have to do it.

I soon learned that the number of kitchen staff had been cut back since the high and heady days of the old 9th Earl's time. Where once there had been two kitchen maids there was now only one: Doris Jones was her name and she was one of the first of the servants I met that day. Everything in the house ran to a strict clock. Doris's day began at 6.30am, when she washed and dressed, tied her hair neatly back and pushed it underneath her little white cap. By 7am she had to have made her bed and be down in the kitchen. It was her job to get breakfast ready for all the servants and begin preparing the early-morning tea trays for the master and mistress, as well as making the children's breakfast.

By 7.30am Winnie Sapsford, who was both cook and housekeeper – another sign that the Coventry finances were coming under increasing strain – arrived in the kitchen. Every television drama you see about life below stairs portrays the cook as a plump and matronly woman. Winnie wasn't like that at all and on that first morning I must admit I was taken back a bit by the look of her. For a start, she was terribly thin: a little bird-like creature that a breath of wind could have blown over. As I looked around the kitchen, with its huge heavy pots and pans, I wondered how she would be able even to lift an empty one, let alone handle it when it was full. I never knew how old she was – she was probably in her late forties or early fifties – but, to my young eyes, she seemed like an archetypical old maid. The scullery maid and Doris the kitchen maid treated her with the greatest of respect – I think they even had to curtsy when she came into the kitchen first thing of a morning – and they always called her 'Mrs Sapsford'. But, in truth, there was never a Mr Sapsford because Winnie had never married. She'd been at the Court for many years and I suppose everyone called her Mrs as a mark of respect.

At 8.45am sharp, breakfast was to be put out on the big table in the servants' hall. But from that first morning I was told that I wouldn't be taking my meals there – and nor would Winnie. It turned out that she and I were one of four members of the household who were termed 'head servants': we were one rung below the Coventry family and – depending on who you compared us to – some levels above the rest of the staff.

Only the lower staff ate in the servants' hall. While they sat down to their breakfast there, us more senior employees were waited upon by the kitchen maid in a room all of our own. The steward's room (I never quite worked out why it was called this) was further along the long echoing main corridor in the basement: this was the arterial heart of all the comings and goings below stairs and the cold stone flags would ring with footsteps as the day's work unfolded.

The four of us who were set apart in the steward's room were Winnie, myself, the children's governess and, the grandest of us all, the butler. Alfred Latter had been in the Coventry's service for more years than anyone cared to remember: he was in his mid to late forties and he ran a strict household, I can tell you. The whole smooth running of the house was ultimately up to him and, if the family ever had any cause for complaint, it would be his ears that heard it and he who took the blame – at least until he got downstairs again.

The moment Mr Latter walked in I was in awe of him. He was immaculately smart, in dark striped trousers and a black jacket over the crispest of crisp white shirts. Although he was only around Dad's age, he looked altogether much more severe and forbidding. Yet, as I sat there, trying to keep out of sight as best as I could, he turned to me with a smile and spoke a few words, which instantly put me at my ease and made me think that, perhaps, he might turn out to be a great deal more kindly than he looked.

'Miss Mulley,' he said in a quiet yet authoritative voice, 'I know exactly how you feel. Please don't worry: you will be very welcome here with us.'

Well, I didn't know whether to smile in relief or burst out crying again. I had passed such a miserable night and, if truth be told, I was feeling just as lonely and frightened in the light of day as I had when I'd gone up to bed. And just as I had been wondering how I could possibly come to terms with life as a servant – albeit a privileged one – the most important man below stairs had taken the trouble to put me at my ease. I could have hugged him.

Throughout the course of that first day I was gradually introduced to the rest of the staff. Under Mr Latter was a footman and a pantry boy, sometimes known as a hallboy. The way it worked was that a lad went into service at the age of around 14 (just as soon as he'd got a basic education, so that he could read and write and do simple arithmetic): he'd start out as a hallboy, which meant looking after the butler's clothes and basically being his dogsbody. For the hallboy (and for all the under servants, for that matter), Mr Latter was as close as you could get to God. The next level up was footman, and hallboys were meant to gradually work their way up to this less lowly position: how long it took really depended on the ability and intelligence of the boy in question – as well as how quickly the person above him got promoted or moved on to service in another great household.

The footman's duties were just as onerous as the kitchen maid's, though in different ways and parts of the house. Below stairs he was expected to clean and polish all the silverware – cutlery, of course, but ornamental objects such as candlesticks and anything else that might be used by the family on a daily basis – all under Mr Latter's stern gaze and precise direction. I would, before long, see how this worked in action and get a glimpse of the very serious security measures Mr Latter imposed.

Upstairs the footman would be required to wait upon the Earl and the Countess at breakfast, lunch and dinner. And if they had guests – as most great families often did – there was far too much for one footman to do. There had once, I gathered, been three footmen employed at Crome Court but it was another sign of the straitened times that their number had been whittled down to just one. So, whenever there was a dinner party or other entertainment going on in the reception rooms upstairs, Roland – the chauffeur who had met me from the station – would be pressed into service as a second footman.

Now, I've said there was a social divide between the head servants and those classified as beneath them – and it was a pretty strict divide, I can tell you. But there was another demarcation line in the servants' quarters and that was sex: the people under Mr Latter's direct control were all men, while the female staff all reported to Winnie. In addition to her two skivvies (as I came to think of them) in the kitchen, there were two housemaids – one senior, one junior. It was the more junior one who had woken me up that morning with a cup of tea and the news that I had a hot bath ready and waiting. Her name, it turned out, was Miriam and, since I can't remember much about her at all, I rather think that she must have been told to mind her Ps and Qs around me because I was a head servant.

The head housemaid – who was in charge of the other two and reported directly to Winnie – was Elizabeth Burridge. She treated me well and with respect but I didn't get the sense that I would have an ally in her. However, the second housemaid, Dorothy Clark, was a different kettle of fish and I sensed from that first morning that she and I would get on. Believe me, I was very much in need of a friend in this vast, strange house and just a few minutes chatting with Dorothy in between her numerous duties made me think that I had found one.

Does all this talk of head servants and lesser staff, of hierarchies and a social order within a social order make your head spin? It's very different to the world we know now, of course, and I shouldn't blame you if you scratched your head and wondered what it was all for and why it had to be all so formal. The reason I shouldn't blame you at all is because that's exactly what I was thinking as the day wore on. Goodness, what a carry-on it all was: I didn't feel so much like a fish out of water as one who has been filleted, dressed and served up on one of the big silver platters Mr Latter kept safely under lock and key!

And all of this was just downstairs. I hadn't even met my mistress yet – much less begun to find out precisely what my duties were to be. But that wasn't to last too much longer. Late in the afternoon Mr Latter came downstairs and told me that her Ladyship wanted to see me in her boudoir. I'd barely time to wonder what a boudoir might be, or the difference between this and a bedroom, when I was led up the big stone steps to the family's rooms on the second floor. A firm yet respectful knock on a closed door and Mr Latter left me alone, waiting to be summonsed into my employer's presence. And I wished the floor – which I somehow registered as being richly carpeted – would open up and swallow me, Mr Latter, Dorothy, Winnie and the whole house full of servants and gentry all in one go.

Chapter Six

Addressing and Dressing Milady

'Come.'

The voice was firm and confident: not loud but it carried and what it carried most of all was strength. With my stomach full of butterflies I opened the door and saw Nesta, Countess of Coventry sitting at her dressing table.

It must have been around 5pm because she was beginning to get herself ready for dinner. She stood up as I walked across the room and the first thing that struck me was how tall she was. I'm only a little shrimp – five foot nothing, just like Mum and Dad – and the Countess towered above me. She must have been six feet if she was an inch. That's tall even today but 80 years ago people in Britain were shorter than they are now – I think the national diet wasn't as good back then – and so Lady Coventry's height was even more unusual.

The next thing I noticed was her hair: it was thick and black and wavy and, my goodness, it was long. I must have looked like a star-struck girl but I was astonished to see that it came all the way down her back to her waist. Just as this was going through my head it dawned on me that I hadn't the faintest idea how to address my new mistress, nor what she would call me. But the Countess soon sorted that out.

'Welcome, Mulley,' she said and I saw quickly how things were going to be: no first names, no Miss Mulley – I was to be known just by my last name from now on. And if that wasn't enough to let me know my place, the next sentence certainly was.

'You will address me as "Milady", Mulley. Not "Lady Coventry", or "Your Ladyship" – always "Milady". Do you understand?'

I nodded dumbly.

'Your duties are to help me with anything I need. You will be in charge of my wardrobe.'

I looked around the room, looking for a big wooden cupboard, but couldn't see one: what was I supposed to do with a wardrobe? And how, since there didn't seem to be one visible? If she saw my confusion, my mistress didn't show it but, in any event, moved swiftly on to an explanation.

'You will be responsible for my clothes, Mulley: you will get my day clothes ready each evening and, while I bathe the next morning, you will lay them out for me on the bed. On the days when I am going to hounds I shall be up very early, so you must lay my hunting attire out the night before and have a bath ready on my return with freshly laundered day wear for me to put on afterwards.'

Well, that was a first for me: I'd never heard the phrase 'going to hounds', nor been involved in anything to do with hunting, and had to make a bit of a leap to guess that she was apparently talking about chasing after foxes. I hoped I wasn't expected to have anything to do with that! 'Every morning – whether I go hunting or not – and every afternoon, I shall require you to brush my hair. One full hour in the morning and one half hour before dinner.'

I stole another look at her flowing tresses: didn't the gentry ever brush their own hair? How strange. Still, it plainly wasn't my place to say anything, so I just nodded.

'Now, can you cut hair?'

Well, I was about to say yes, that everyone of my class and upbringing knew how to chop the ends of each other's hair and generally make it look respectable – no fancy hairdressers for us. But something made me realise that hacking away at my sister's locks wasn't quite the same thing as trimming and styling the hair of a Countess: I shook my head.

'Oh. Well, we shall just have to send you for training. You can, of course, sew and make clothes – that was your trade, wasn't it?'

Here I knew I was on firmer ground and answered, with an inner confidence, even if outwardly I was quaking in my sensible shoes.

'Yes, Milady. I'm a trained dressmaker and tailor. I can take care of anything which needs repairing and make any clothes you would like.'

'Good. You will also look after my jewellery: keep it clean and polished and, of course, be responsible for its safe-keeping.'

'Oh Lord,' I thought. 'Now you know you've landed amongst the gentry. She's bound to have whole boxes of fabulously valuable jewels – diamonds and tiaras and suchlike – and you're responsible for every one of them. Heaven help you if one of them gets damaged or goes missing: you'll be out on your ear before you can say sorry.'

'I will show you where everything is tomorrow,' she continued. 'But as to your wages: you will be paid five shillings a week. Mr Latter will see to everything.'

Well, five shillings didn't sound very much at all – though I suppose it was five times what I'd earned at Mrs King's dressmaking business. But then I realised that, as well as my wages, I'd be fed and watered – I wouldn't have to pay a penny for my keep – and I'd be living in one of the greatest houses in England. I wouldn't have minded a few bob more, don't get me wrong but, as I mentally added things up, I realised that five shillings and all found (as we used to call it) meant that I'd be able to send some money home to Mum and Dad.

'That will be all, Mulley. Oh – you don't have to wear a uniform. You are, after all, head staff, but please make sure you wear dark clothes and, when you brush my hair, you must wear a pinny. Ms Sapstead will see to that for you.'

With that, I was dismissed from my mistress's presence. She turned away from me and picked up a beautiful long evening dress – I didn't recognise the exact fabric but I knew enough to know that it was worth many times my weekly wages – she was to wear to dinner.

'Excuse me, Milady, but is there anything else I can do for you?' I asked in what sounded a very small voice. 'It's just that I don't know what to do when I'm not wanted.'

The Countess turned back to me. She was, as I hope you've gathered by now, really quite a frightening figure. How on earth had I plucked up the courage to speak to her?

'Do?' she asked, as if tasting and testing an unfamiliar concept. 'I have no idea what you will do: you are to be my lady's maid and that means you will do whatever I need you to do, whenever I need it. As for anything else,' – she waved her hand vaguely at me – 'well, I imagine your time is your own.'

'Well, goodness,' I thought. 'That's me told. I won't make that mistake again in a hurry, that's for certain.' I gave my best imitation of a curtsey and fled as fast as decorum would allow. In the relative safety of the steward's room I flopped down into a chair and went over my first encounter with Her Ladyship in my mind. This was my first taste of service and it was without doubt one of the rummest experiences in my life. Still, I was here, I was employed and I'd better make the best of it: that's what I told myself, although inside I wanted to curl up into a ball and then roll all the way back to Stamford and Vine Street and Mum, Dad, Joan and Jim.

In the end it was Dorothy Clark who came to my rescue. Although she was really only Second Housemaid – and so was termed one of the under servants – she had been looking after Lady Coventry since her previous lady's maid had retired after many years of service.

'Don't you worry about Her Ladyship,' Dorothy told me as I sat, still trembling, in the chair. 'You just treat her with respect and she'll treat you the same way. Or at least with as much respect as one of the gentry ever treats their servants!'

It was good advice and would, in time, serve me well. But at that moment I was still completely overwhelmed by the whole business. There was never any doubt that I would treat my new mistress with the utmost respect: she was far too frightening a figure to do otherwise. But whether she would ever come to warm enough to me for there to be anything more than the most formal of relationships – well, on that score I definitely had my doubts.

Dorothy, though, was full of comforting information and advice and I quickly sensed that here was someone who could not just teach me the ropes but with whom I could be friends. She was about my own age, pretty and vivacious. I immediately warmed to her and thought, 'Here's someone who will be a pal.' And let me tell you, I had never felt as much in need of a pal as I did that day. But no sooner had the thought entered my head than Dorothy told me something that sent my heart sinking down again.

'You need to remember that you're a head servant. There are pretty strict rules about the way things are done here and one of those rules is that head servants aren't supposed to mix much with us lower ones. You're expected to keep yourself to yourself – a bit aloof, like. Friendships aren't really encouraged here and, because you're one level higher than me, you'll be expected to socialise only with your equals.'

I'd never come across anything like this in my life. Where I came from, people were people and it didn't matter who they were or what their station in life was: if they were friendly to you, you were friendly right back at them. But here in this great house the game was played very differently, it seemed. All of us beneath stairs were, of course, expected to know our place when it came to the family: but now I discovered that there were different rungs on our already very limited social ladder.

As I've said, the head servants (apart from me) were the butler, the housekeeper-cook and the children's governess. Well, I'd already seen that Mr Latter was very much top of the tree and he plainly wasn't going to be a friend I could confide in, much less one with whom I could really socialise. Don't get me wrong, he was a good man and kind but, to rise to the position of butler, he had learned the hierarchy of service in the days when it was even more strict – he would have had to have spent at least a decade gradually rising through the ranks, from a start as the lowliest of footmen. Now he was the most senior servant in the house and his very position meant that he had to keep a good deal of distance between himself and the rest of us.

Nor was the governess any more promising. Mrs Lovett was her name and, in truth, she kept even more to herself than Mr Latter. In many ways, I suppose, this was inevitable. Her domain was the children's nursery and the schoolroom and she would often take her meals there with her charges, so I didn't see terribly much of her.

That left Winnie Sapsford, the housekeeper-cook. Her

position in itself was slightly unusual. Most great houses like Croome Court would have employed both a cook and a housekeeper – certainly the 9th Earl did and, since he and the late Countess were great ones for entertaining, the cook would have been kept pretty busy just keeping up with the demands made on the kitchen, let alone supervising all the household staff and managing the daily routine of cleaning, washing, ironing and the like. Although I didn't quite realise it then, the fact that Winnie was doing both jobs was a sign that the Coventry finances were not in the healthiest of shapes.

I think I liked Winnie from the off: certainly she never did me any harm, nor made my life anything but bearable. She made sure that I always had enough to eat and drink. But I'd sensed something about her on our first meeting: I couldn't put my finger on what it was, but I realised that whilst we would get on just fine, she was never going to be what I could call a friend. All in all, things on that front weren't looking at all promising.

Looking back, I can see why the servants' structure – with its rigid demarcations and prohibitions on friendships – was the way it was. In some ways, working below stairs in a great house must be like being in the army: everyone has to know their orders and be prepared both to give or receive them without the possibility of them being questioned. Friendships between the giver of orders and the person to whom they were issued make it less easy for obedience, I suppose. It's that old idea of familiarity breeding contempt.

'Hey ho,' I thought to myself. 'This is a funny sort of place you've come to, and no mistake. Hilda, my girl, you'll just have to grin and bear it and make the best of everything.' It's funny to look back on the way things were then but, in some way, Croome Court was a microcosm of England itself between the two world wars. People grew up knowing their station in life (now there's a phrase you don't hear today) and were brought up not just to know their place but to accept it. There's another phrase that you used to hear all the time in those days: 'Mustn't grumble.' It was the standard answer to anyone – at least anyone of your own class; you'd never dream of saying anything so casual to your 'betters' – who might ask you how you were, or how your work day had been. 'Mustn't grumble,' we said and we meant it: we were expected never to grumble about anything because that was all part of the English way. And, like the phrase itself, that's a way that was blown away by the Second World War.

As my first full day in service came to its somewhat gloomy end, if anyone had asked me how it had gone (of course no one did!), I'd most likely have answered, 'Mustn't grumble.' But when I went to bed that night, I cried and cried until at last I fell asleep.

I was woken the next day at 7am by Miriam, the third housemaid, bearing a cup of tea and telling me she'd run my bath: apparently, yesterday hadn't been a one-off but was to be the way all of my days would start. Well, I thought, that's a bit of luck, anyway: no one had ever brought me a cup of tea in bed before and it seemed that, in Miriam, I was to have my very own servant. But the next thing she said made it clear that this was to be the only luxurious part of my daily routine.

'Please, Miss Mulley, you're to have your bath and dress and be downstairs at seven-thirty. Mrs Sapstead has done you an egg and some toast but she will have Her Ladyship's tea ready for you by then, so she says you've to be quick about your breakfast. It doesn't do to be late for Her Ladyship.'

So this was how it was to be. There's an old saying we used to learn in school: 'Big fleas have little fleas upon their backs to bite them. And little fleas have littler fleas and so on *ad infinitum*.' I felt like one of the middle fleas – privileged up to a point but only so long as the 'big flea' was happy. Still, I enjoyed my cup of tea, slipped into my dressing gown and padded along the corridor to find that the bath was delightfully piping hot.

I'd hung my clothes up in the wardrobe as soon as I arrived but, when I went to get my dress for my first full morning in service, my heart sank again. The wardrobe was huge and my few garments looked so sparse and lonely that I once again felt a pang of homesickness. Not that I would have had any more clothes but at least they wouldn't have looked so, well, inadequate.

I'd also been forewarned about what sort of clothes to bring. As a head servant, I didn't have to wear a uniform like the housemaids or the footmen: instead, I was told that Her Ladyship expected me to wear dark colours. Now, my favourite colours were green and purple – I've always loved them and do so still. But at Croome Court such cheerful hues were not allowed and so the dresses hanging in the big mahogany wardrobe looked even more depressing than they might.

By the time I was bathed, clothed and ready to face the day it was almost 7.30am. I rushed down the three flights of stone stairs and positively burst into the kitchen. Everything there seemed to be chaotically busy, with Winnie presiding over her scullery staff as they boiled and grilled amid great clouds of steam and smoke. A tray was set on a table in one corner and no sooner had I arrived than a cup of tea was placed upon it and the whole lot was thrust into my hands with an upward jerk of a thumb to indicate that I needed to get it to Her Ladyship on the double. Back I went up the great stone steps – rather more carefully this time as I juggled the tea, a folded linen napkin and a little flower vase on the slippery tray.

When I got to my mistress's door, I had a moment of panic: did I just knock and enter? Or wait to be summonsed? And would Her Ladyship be in bed with the Earl? Did they even share a bedroom? I knew from stories I'd read that lots of the gentry slept separately, only ever coming together to go about the business of producing heirs.

Would the Coventrys be like this? And if they weren't, was I prepared for the sight of His Lordship in bed? You have to remember that life was very much more sheltered in those days and I don't think I'd ever seen a man in his nightclothes. I knocked on the heavy oak door and tried to stop my heart beating so fast that it seemed likely to jump out of my chest and knock the whole tea tray flying.

In the end, my fears were groundless: I heard the deep rich voice of the Countess – 'Come' – and marched in to find her sitting up in bed alone. Now, at this point I should probably tell you a little bit about the arrangement of the family's quarters on the second floor. If you go to Croome Court today – and since it's part of the National Trust and open to the public, I really think you should – you'll see that on either side of the Earl and Countess's bedroom there are doors leading off into other rooms. In my day these were the Earl's dressing room on one side and the Countess's boudoir on the other. As I was to discover, as soon as he heard my knock on the door, the Earl would get up and retreat into his dressing room while I saw to my mistress's needs alone. I never did know whether he got a cup of tea delivered to him there: I certainly never brought him one and I never saw anyone else with a tray, so I rather think he missed out.

I plumped up the pillows behind Her Ladyship's elegant shoulders while she adjusted a beautiful silk nightgown. In my dressmaking apprenticeship I'd seen some lovely fabric, even though we weren't making clothes for the gentry, but I could see straight away that what the Countess was wearing was of a different class all together. Well, I said to myself, if this is what she puts on to go to bed, what will the rest of her outfits be like? Of course, those outfits were one of the main parts of my duties. While her ladyship drank her tea, I first nipped off down the corridor to her private bathroom and began the process of drawing hot water for her to bathe in. When that was done, my mistress got herself up, took the dressing gown (another piece of lovely material) I held out for her and told me what she wanted to wear that day. It was my job to lay all of her clothes out on the bed – every last stitch she would wear – in the order in which she would put them on.

Now, maybe you're thinking that doesn't sound like much: after all, everybody wears clothes and surely it couldn't have been very different back then? But it was: it most certainly was. You see the way we dress now bears very little resemblance to what a lady would wear in

1935. For a start, there was a great deal more in the way of underwear.

The first thing a lady put on would, of course, be her knickers. These were nothing like the sort of panties that you buy today: they were big, baggy silk things you stepped into and which came down to somewhere between the calf and the knee, and what they lacked in being flattering to the figure I suppose they made up for in terms of comfort. In themselves, these garments were a fairly new invention: until the 1920s, ladies' knickers were open between the legs, which must have made them somewhat draughty.

But it was the next item of under clothing that seems outlandish to people today. The modern bra was only invented in 1913 and, by the time I was tending to Her Ladyship, it was very definitely not in widespread use. Instead, she, like most women, wore a sort of complicated corset known as a girdle: this combined a basic brassiere with an elasticated middle section – to compress the tummy and waist into a slim, narrow shape – to which were attached straps for keeping up stockings. These, like the girdle itself, would be made of rayon. Now, I don't think most people today have ever heard of rayon – or if they have, they won't know what it was – but before the Second World War it was used for just about every sort of women's clothing, and especially underwear. It's really a sort of halfway house between completely natural fibres like wool or cotton and the synthetic materials we take for granted today. Nylon, for example, wasn't even invented until 1935 and it wasn't until American soldiers brought nylon stockings to Britain after 1942 that women here ever saw it. Of course, tights hadn't even been thought of then, so rayon stockings were what everyone was used to and it was known to common people like me as 'artificial silk' because that's how it felt on the skin.

On top of all this, there would also be a slip and possibly a petticoat before the whole complicated business was hidden from view with a dress. Trousers were, in theory, a possibility but in those inter-war years only what we called 'fast women' really wore them: they were seen as something not really respectable and it would take the war – when women were pressed into service in industry, on the land or in the forces – before they lost their rather risqué image.

When Her Ladyship disappeared to bathe, my duties began in earnest. I would first tidy and prepare the various pots of face preparation, powders and other make-up on her dressing table. An aristocratic lady like the Countess would never dream of keeping her own dressing table clean and tidy: that was my job, every morning and evening. Next, I would go into her boudoir to collect up what she had been wearing the day before. Mostly this would be her evening wear – for in those days ladies dressed formally for dinner. The Countess had some truly beautiful evening dresses, made of the most gorgeous and expensive materials but, in the way of things back then, she would simply shed these when she came up for bed, leaving them in a higgledy-piggledy mess on the floor. I bundled up the garments that would need to be washed and carefully folded the rest to take back to my room. Here I would press them to within an inch of their lives so that they looked as good as new (despite their night on the floor), ready to be worn again that evening if Her Ladyship so chose.

And then, once my mistress returned from her bath, I would help dress her in whatever outfit she had chosen for the day. Now, if all of this makes the Countess seem very pernickety, it's only fair to point out that, by reputation, she was a great deal less fussy about what she wore than most ladies of her station. In fact, I was horrified to hear from Dorothy that it was far from unknown for Milady to wear the same dirty pair of knickers several days in a row: that was not the way I'd been brought up – and the Mulleys of Stamford had a great deal less money (not to mention a rather more basic method of laundry) than the Coventrys of Croome Court. It just goes to show, I told myself, that money isn't everything in this world.

Then came the part of the morning that I would come to dread: brushing my mistress's hair. She had, of course, warned me about this but, even so, I found this morning ritual to be terribly tiring and distinctly boring. I wonder, do you ever take the time to calculate how long you spend brushing your hair of a morning? I rather think that most of us won't spend more than a minute or so – unless we're using some of those fancy hair tongs or straighteners that young girls seem so keen on today. There weren't any such things back in the 1930s: the only tool I had at my disposal was Her Ladyship's silver-backed hairbrush – that and good old elbow grease. So I stood there behind her as she readied herself for the ritual. Brush, brush, brush – and then brush again. Stroke after stroke, minute after minute until the full hour – and believe me, Milady timed me – of brushing had been accomplished. My feet ached from standing still so long and my brushing arm felt ready to drop off by the time I'd finished and my mistress had declared herself satisfied. Then, and only then, was I dismissed from her presence.

And what, do you suppose, the Earl was doing all this time? From the moment I'd knocked on the door with his wife's morning cup of tea he was nowhere to be seen. The answer turned out to be that he was receiving very much the same sort of treatment from Mr Latter: the whole routine with the clothes (though not, I think, with the hair brushing, since His Lordship sported the short back and sides of all respectable gentlemen). But, incredible as it may seem to us today, both of these grown adults – and Her

Ladyship was almost twice my age – were apparently unable to decide for themselves what clothes to put on of a morning, much less to get themselves dressed on their own.

At 9.30am the Earl and Countess descended the big stone staircase and settled themselves in the dining room to take breakfast. As a lady's maid, I never saw what went on in there – although I would see Winnie and her kitchen maids working up whole silver salvers of bacon, eggs, devilled kidneys, kedgeree and the like: it was the footmen and Mr Latter who waited on the family when they took their meals and, though we weren't meant to gossip about the family, I soon found out that, before they ever undid a napkin or plunged a knife into the butter, the Earl said prayers. And when he finished, Her Ladyship would add her own appeal to the Almighty: 'God, make my servants dutiful.' Since there was no 'please' in that sentence, I realised not only that our duties were a matter of the strictest requirement but that the aristocracy were evidently on first-name terms with God.

There was one other very noticeable aspect to the Earl and the Countess's breakfasts: they took them alone. By the time I joined the household in August 1935, the Coventrys had four children: three daughters and one son. The eldest, at 13, was Lady Anne; next came Lady Joan, aged 11, then Lady Maria, who was 4, and the youngest of all was George William (the family always called their first sons by those names), who was barely 18 months and known to everyone simply as Bill. Lady Anne and Lady Joan had been dispatched to boarding school and were thus away from Croome for much of the year but, even in school holidays, neither they nor the two youngsters ate with their parents.

Coming from a close family such as mine where, even had there been room enough in the little cottage to send the three of us children to eat on our own, my parents would never have considered it. The way the Coventrys brought up their children seemed very odd to me. They rarely saw them from one day to the next: most often, their only contact would be for a few minutes after the children had eaten their supper and were brought down to speak to their parents before being whisked back up to their playroom. Even at bedtime it was Mrs Lovett who supervised everything and tucked them in for the night. To my mind, it didn't bode well: even though I was just 19, I had enough about me to suspect that this very aristocratic way of family life might one day reap some less than respectable rewards. Little did I know how tragically that premonition was to be realised.

Chapter Seven

Exploring Croome Court

It took a week for me to stop crying myself to sleep at night.

The days themselves began to resolve into some sort of routine: up at 7am, drink tea, have bath, rush down the three flights of stairs, gulp down breakfast then whisk Milady's tray upstairs and begin work on her daily needs. I found my way to the laundry – a huge bustling place where all the family's bedding was washed and ironed every morning ready for the housemaids to make up again in the afternoon. I set up an ironing board in my bedroom so that I could press the Countess's clothes. It was a relief to discover that I had an electric socket in my room and was issued with an electric iron: a vast improvement on the heavy old cast-iron implements I was used to at home.

I suppose that, if I'd wanted it, Miriam, the third housemaid who seemed to be looking after me, would have made up my bed for me. But I'd been brought up by Mum's strict standards and I couldn't bear to allow someone else to do this for me. The bedding, of course, was the old-fashioned type: no duvets in those days! And so every morning I started the bed from scratch and made sure the sheets were put back, neat as a new pin with hospital corners, just as Mum had taught me. Standards were important to Mum and, just because I'd landed in a place where I was treated as a superior being by the other servants, I wasn't going to let them drop away.

Once Her Ladyship had breakfasted she would often return to her boudoir. She would summon me and give me my instructions for the day ahead and tell me what she wanted to wear for dinner in the evening. In those first few days it was just like that: firm instructions with no question of asking my opinion. But towards the end of the first week she seemed to thaw a little and for the first time spoke to me as if I was someone who might have something useful to say.

'What do you think I should wear tonight, Mulley?' was the first advice she sought from me one day. Well, I had only barely begun to comprehend the enormity of her wardrobe. It seemed to be absolutely stuffed with the most impossibly lovely gowns – mostly long but with a number of very fashionable shorter cocktail dresses. I'd no idea what was required of an Earl's wife when it came to evening dress and, at first, I played safe by suggesting either what I knew she had already worn or at least something similar. It would take a fair while before I felt confident that I knew enough to give any proper advice.

Then there were her jewels. In the corner of the boudoir was Milady's safe. On my second morning with her she handed me a little key and told me I was to be responsible for laying out the jewellery she would wear in the evening, making sure it was clean and sparkling and that it matched whatever gown she had chosen to wear. Can you imagine my nervousness when I took the little key into my hand? Here was I, a 19-year-old girl earning just £13 a year, being handed the key to a safe that must hold tens of thousands of pounds' worth of diamonds and pearls.

The first time I opened the safe her Ladyship stood beside me and took out a typed list of all that was in there. But I only had eyes for the precious stones, gold rings and sparkling necklaces: it was like finding Aladdin's cave tucked discreetly in the corner of the room. The Countess must have seen my face and, in her mind, I suppose, tried to put me at my ease.

'These aren't the valuable ones, Mulley. I don't keep them here. These are just the ordinary ones for everyday wear.'

Well, all I knew what that what I saw before me – what I was now in charge of – were the most beautiful things I had ever seen. If these were only the less precious ones, what on earth could the real treasures look like? I made a mental note to talk to Mr Latter about the whole business. It wasn't too long before I had the chance to do just that. Bless him, he must have seen how anxious I was and he patiently explained the situation.

'The Countess keeps only her less valuable jewels here. Some of it might, I think, be classed as costume jewellery and, however brightly it sparkles, it might not really be made of genuine stones. Nonetheless, since she has given you the key to the safe, you are legally responsible for its safe-keeping, and you must understand that Her Ladyship has placed a great trust in you.'

That didn't exactly bolster my confidence. What if something should go missing? What if somehow someone got in and stole from the safe? What would happen to me? Would I be arrested and taken to prison? I should certainly lose my position – that much was beyond doubt. I gulped.

'You must try not to worry yourself about this, Miss Mulley,' Mr Latter continued. 'I know you will do very well for Her Ladyship and I have every confidence that the trust she has placed in you will be fulfilled.' His face relaxed into a smile and, in a manner that came as close to conspiratorial as his training and position would allow, he

Above Left: A portrait of me taken in 1937.

Above Right: Me, my sister Joan, my brother Jim and our dog, Jock.

Below Left: Here I am at the age of 20, a year after starting at Croome Court.

Below Right: The Servants' Ball was an exciting occasion for us in the household, and I made my own dress for it, trimmed with white 'fur'.

In the grounds at Croome Court, relaxing by the fishing lake.

Nesta Donne Phillips, the Countess and my mistress.

I'm very proud of this picture – it is not often that a servant was allowed to take a picture of the family, and Mr Latter was quite shocked by it!

One of the wonderful results of my time at Croome Court was meeting Roland. We were married in Stamford on 15 June 1940 and although we were in the midst of war we were so happy just to be together.

Above: Lady Coventry and I volunteered to join the Auxiliary Territorial Service together and, for the first time in five years, we were separated in order to 'do our bit'.

Below Left: Roland – my Roll.

Above Left: Lord and Lady Coventry at the United Counties Show in Camarthen, Wales.

Above Right: The two youngest children, Maria and George, with their mother a few years after I joined the household.

Below: This is a picture from the previous Lord and Lady Coventry's Diamond Wedding anniversary, as I described in chapter two.

Croome Court as it stands today. It is now being wonderfully managed by the National Trust which is currently undertaking an extensive restoration programme on the property.

© David Bagnall/Rex Features

leaned towards me and whispered, 'Her Ladyship's real jewellery is far away from here. It is kept in a vault in one of the oldest and most secure banks in London – so that should be a weight off your mind. And as for Croome Court: well, let me show you something.'

He led me through the corridors of the servants' quarter and into his own sanctuary, the Butler's Parlour. This room, I knew, was where he spent those parts of the day when he wasn't attending to the family's needs and fulfilling the duties of valet to the Earl. It was a very large room – larger even than my bedroom – and one whole wall was lined with sinks. This was where – under Mr Latter's strict supervision – the lower footmen washed up the fine porcelain and silver cutlery that the Coventrys used for dining. There was a big coal range in the corner, gleaming with blackleading, on the sides of which were two oblong containers: these were where the fire heated the water, which would then be carried over in pans to the sinks. In the top of one wall there was a long glass panel that would have been at ground level on the outside of the front of the house. This was how the butler was able to see who was arriving at the Court in time to get upstairs and open the great front door to welcome them.

But what Mr Latter wanted to show me was a huge, heavy cast-iron door in the opposite wall. This really looked like something out of a Victorian prison.

'This, Miss Mulley, is the strong room. In here we keep all the family's silver – a collection much more valuable than the jewels for which you are responsible. Much more valuable by a very long chalk, Miss Mulley.'

As he continued, I began to understand just how cleverly Croome Court had been designed and built. There was, of course, only one door to the strong room and, as Mr Latter pulled it open, I could see just how heavy and secure it was. Inside, the ceiling was of a completely different design to anything else I had seen in the house. The bedrooms all had straightforward – if very high – ceilings and those for the servants' quarters downstairs were arched. But the ceiling in the strong room was a complex series of mini-arches, intersecting and giving the room a very odd feel indeed. Nor was this an accident.

When Capability Brown and Robert Adam were rebuilding Croome Court 200 years earlier, they knew that gentry such as the Earl of Coventry would possess many thousands of pounds' worth of silver and gold – the equivalent to millions of pounds today. And they knew that, in the lawless and poverty-ridden conditions of the time – when police forces hadn't even been invented – this treasure would act like a magnet for burglars. I discovered that the favourite technique of house cracksmen (as burglars were known) was to dig their way into a strong room from above, and so, between them, the creators of

Croome designed a ceiling with multiple vaults and in-built strengths to ensure that any burglar would find it almost impossible to crack.

Nor was that the only security precaution. Every evening the strong room was locked shut – Mr Latter had the only key – and a cot bed was placed against it, just inside the butler's pantry. On this bed, one or other of the footmen took turns to sleep, so that it would be impossible for anyone even to approach the strong room door without waking him up.

Well, of course, I was impressed and (as Mr Latter had no doubt intended) really quite reassured about the onerous burden of taking responsibility for Milady's jewels. But I couldn't help thinking how uncomfortable and cold it must be to spend the night on a little cot in the butler's pantry. And I began to realise that, in many ways, I was being very well treated.

For a start, I was never hungry. Not only were all my meals provided – hot and nourishing and made for me – but Winnie Sapstead was always very generous, making sure I was provided with cake of an afternoon. We began to settle into a little routine where I would take the bits of sewing and mending the Countess had given me to do into the steward's room and Winnie would bring up something additional for me to do – sew a button on a uniform here, or mend a tear there. In return, she would be armed with a bit of fruit loaf or something she had made for the family. If nothing else, I was definitely getting more than crumbs from the gentry's table.

Although Croome Court itself was always fearsomely cold – don't forget it was a vast, cavernous place and there was no such thing as central heating in those days – my bedroom was always kept supplied with my very own bucket of coal. I knew from the snatches of gossip of the other servants below stairs that not all fine families treated their servants like this and that having an unrestricted supply of coal – no questions asked about how much I used – was a sign that the Coventrys took great care of their servants.

Still, it wasn't home. After I had laid out my mistress's clothes for the evening and helped her dress for dinner (I'd polished up her diamonds and pearls ready for her to choose what to wear), I would largely be left to my own devices. And warm though my bedroom might be, in the flickering gas light of an evening I was terribly homesick. And that's why I cried myself to sleep.

During the day I was kept busy enough not to feel too low and, within weeks of starting my position, I began my hairdressing course. The place where I was to be trained was in Worcester – nearly ten miles away. Croome Court was, as I have explained, in a very isolated position in the countryside and, while there was a bus service from right outside the London Arch, it only ran once a day and was plainly not going to be suitable. Instead, the Countess instructed that the family chauffeur was to ferry me back and forth for my once-a-week lessons.

Roland Newman had been the first of the staff that I'd met and – although I never said as much to him and probably didn't even admit it to myself – I'd been rather taken by him. He was good looking and had tried to be friendly and, if he was a little older than me, in those days that was much less of a concern than it seems to be today. And so I was secretly rather looking forward to being chauffeured to Worcester. I did, though, hope we might have a rather better means of transport than that with which I had been met on my arrival.

Sadly, this wasn't to be. The Coventry family owned – and Roland drove for them – a very smart car indeed: not a Rolls-Royce or a Bentley but a very swish Standard 20 with deep red coachwork and the finest leather seats. Over the years many people have commented on this and find it surprising that the Earl hadn't splashed out on a Rolls – after all, in every film or television drama you see about the 1930s the aristocracy is always shown in the biggest and most luxurious Roller. But that's fiction and real life for the Coventrys – especially in the straitened financial climate of the 1930s – was different.

For one thing, the Standard Motor Company was very

much a local enterprise: its cars had been built – sometimes hand-built – in Coventry for more than 30 years and I think the Earl was determined that he should support it. After all, he was the Earl of the town where they were constructed! And although the Standard name has long since disappeared (it was eventually swallowed up into British Leyland as part of the rationalisation of Britain's motor industry in the 1960s and 1970s), before the Second World War it had a very good reputation for reliability and comfort. The Standard 20 was very much the top model in the range.

I'd caught a glimpse of this magnificent machine on the driveway outside and seen Roland open its big solid doors for my mistress and the Earl. And so, naturally, I hoped that this would be the way I would ride into Worcester. Perhaps I was guilty of giving myself a few too many airs and graces with this because, when the time came for Roland to take me to my first lesson, there was the smelly blue hound van again. 'Ah, well,' I told myself. 'That'll teach you to get ideas above your station.'

As it turned out, I didn't really notice the rather basic nature of the vehicle too much – although I did enquire why it was called a hound van. The answer was that the Countess was a very keen huntswoman and that Croome had its own pack of hounds. Not only were these transported to and from meets in the back of the little blue van but it was also used to collect offal and cheap cuts of meat for their daily suppers. This, at least, explained the rather odd smell. But as I say, as the weeks passed, I began to notice less and less about the van and more and more about the quietly dashing Roland Newman. I could also see that he was beginning to take a shine to me. I determined to find out a little more about him and his background.

Roland was, in fact, 11 years older than me. He was one of three brothers and one sister who had grown up in the nearby village of Severn Stoke – well, I say a village but it was really more of a hamlet. His mother and father had been agricultural workers on the Croome estate and lived in a little tied cottage next to the Rose & Crown pub. By the time I met Roland, his parents were retired, although his dad was still the ghillie, acting as a sort of unofficial official on the river. His brother Sid worked at a famous racing stables nearby, while Arnold, the other brother, was living and working on a local farm and Roland lived with them.

Roland had joined the Earl of Coventry's staff several years earlier and, in addition to his duties as a chauffeur (and acting as a part-time footman whenever the local gentry came to dinner), he also looked after the Court's water-pumping station – for a house that size and set in so rural a location had to have its own water works – and helped out with just about anything that any of the other servants needed doing by way of mechanics. I'd discovered – in truth, I'd made it my business to find out – that he was a very popular member of the servants' household. All in all, I began to look forward to our trips to Worcester and to miss his company on the days when I didn't see him.

But, just as my heart was warming to this warm and personable man, my mind sounded a very sharp note of warning. Since you're reading this, I think it's a fair bet that you've watched some of the television programmes about life below stairs. They always seem to have storylines involving various members of the staff getting involved and having love affairs. But that's just television for you because, in my day, romances between servants in the same house were not just frowned on but absolutely forbidden. If friendships between head servants like me and housemaids like Dorothy Clark were actively discouraged, for most of the gentry of the time, an actual relationship between a man and woman in their employ would have been unthinkable.

'Listen, my girl,' I said to myself, 'If this goes any further and you allow these feelings to develop between you and Roland, one or other of us – possibly both – will find ourselves in very hot water indeed. Why, you could even be dismissed on the spot.' And, of course, in those days there was no such thing as employment rights or even a written contract: if your master or mistress decided to give you the sack, you were out on your ear faster than you could say jack rabbit, without so much as a reference, never mind an industrial tribunal.

'You've made your bed, Hilda Mulley,' I thought, 'and you jolly well just better get on and make the best of it.'

With that I made my mind up to abandon any idea of romance with the handsome chauffeur. Instead, I buried myself in improving my relationship with the Countess.

This, in fact, was already beginning to improve. As well as asking my advice on what she should wear each day, as I stood and brushed and rebrushed, my mistress had begun to talk a little more freely about the life at Croome Court. Now, of course, she would never discuss her husband – although I did detect that there was something about His Lordship to be found out – but she talked about her children and it was very clear that she loved them dearly. It must have been terribly difficult for a woman like her to be so separated from her girls and her baby boy, and at the same time to know that they were in the same house. I know it was the tradition and the way the aristocracy had always brought up children but it seemed to me that the Countess was, in some way, just as much a prisoner of her class as I felt in the grandeur of Croome Court. And so, perhaps, chatting to me about her children in some way made her feel closer to them. It wasn't that we were friends

– you could never be friends with someone from such a different class and on whose whims your employment depended – nor that I became her confidante. But I think, in her own way, she came to trust and rely on me both as her servant and – despite my young age – as someone she could talk to.

Occasionally, she would ask about my family and I would tell her a little about growing up in Stamford. After all, if the formality and magnificence of Croome was an alien world to me, the everyday life of working-class people in a small terraced cottage in Lincolnshire must have been like something out of a storybook to Milady.

I wrote to Mum and Dad almost every day and my letters were included in the bundle of post to be taken by a footman (or by Roland) to the nearest post office. I'd tell them about all the comings and goings at Croome, about the hustle and bustle of the servants' hall and about what duties I'd been up to. Mum wrote back to me with news of my sister and my brother, of how Dad's work was going and of day-to-day life in Stamford. All of this I duly imparted to my mistress on such days as she cared to enquire.

She began, too, to grasp that before I had joined her service I had acquired a skill and a training that could be of greater use than simply sewing on buttons and mending rips in her stockings. She began to ask me to make clothes – mainly for the children but sometimes for herself. And I was proud to do so: I felt as though I was making use of my apprenticeship and the £25 Mum had somehow cobbled together to buy me in was at last bearing fruit.

As the summer turned to autumn, that year of 1935, I also began to explore the grounds of my new home. And what grounds they were! From my first venturings out to sit by the river and watch the swallows dart back and forth, snatching midges and mosquitoes off the very surface of the water, I gradually expanded my adventures to the buildings dotted around the estate. Now, when I say this, it really doesn't sound like very much: but if you go to Croome, you will see for yourself just how far I had to walk and how hidden from view these extraordinary pieces of architecture were.

The Court itself had a library and, as befitted a head servant, I was allowed to browse its extensive shelves. Among the many rare volumes was a guidebook, printed more than a hundred years before, which would serve to guide my exploring feet.

Seated on its proud eminence, the Rotunda presents itself to view. It is an elegant stone building; plain in its exterior, but richly ornamented within: furnished with sofas, and fitted up as a summer apartment. A pleasing assemblage of trees, among which are the cypress and the cedar of Lebanon, form with their blended foliage a woody crescent, encircling it and sheltering it. But its great charm is its fine prospect.

Who wouldn't want to explore such a place? I laced up my sensible shoes and set off to the east in search of it. I think it must have taken a good half an hour of steady marching through open parkland and dense shrubbery to track it down. When I did, my first thought was, 'Why would anyone build such a structure?' And the second was, 'What is it for?'

Of course, I was being both silly and sensible all at the same time. The Rotunda – like so many buildings on the estate – wasn't 'for' anything: it had no real purpose and the rich ornamentation promised by the guidebook had long since disappeared – probably for the eminently sensible reason that no one would want to trek for half an hour simply to sit there in splendid isolation. The real reason for the Rotunda, of course, was simply that there was no reason: when it was designed and built, the gentry had a great love of creating what they called (with unabashed accuracy) follies.

'Well,' I thought to myself, 'it must be very good to have the money to put up a fine stone building like this without any use for it.' But if I'm honest, the thought also slipped into my mind that here would be a very fine and private place to sit with a young man, if a girl happened to be courting.

The same rather risky thought crossed my mind on another expedition when I crossed the river and the ha ha – a sort of deep turfed ditch, which split what the guidebook called 'the pleasure grounds' in two – and made my way over the vast expanse of parkland to find the Temple. This turned out to be a truly stunning limestone building, constructed to look like an ancient Greek temple, with six huge columns supporting a frontage on which intricate stone carvings had been sculpted. When it was built, it was intended as a greenhouse and, so I learned, it had vast sash windows to protect the flowers within, while catching and magnifying the sunlight. It also had a highly innovative system of under-floor heating, powered by a brick 'bothy' at the back. It struck me that here was a measure of the eccentricity of the English aristocracy: they would spend a fortune to keep their flowers warm, while the house they and their servants occupied froze them to the bone. It is as they say: the rich are different. But to my mischievous mind, the Temple was admirably remote and just the sort of place where a boy and girl could meet – not, of course, that I would allow any such thing but, if I did, well, this would be quite the location for it.

I think I need to tell you a little bit about courting when I was young enough to think about it. Because times were very, very different then and the more open – not to say forward – way young people behave in our modern world was quite unthinkable in the 1930s. When we – and by that I mean girls and boys of my age – talked about 'courting', it meant nothing more risky than walking out together, talking and – perhaps, once there had been a great deal of walking and a significant amount of talking – occasionally holding hands. Kissing was very much an advanced stage in any budding romance and not to be entered into lightly – at least not by respectable people, and I had been brought up to value respectability. Why, kissing practically meant that you and your chap were engaged – or at least very definitely thinking about that. Certainly no one (or at least no one that I knew) would ever have considered anything more intimate than kissing: sex before marriage was something which, even if was ever mentioned, was spoken of in hushed tones of absolute horror and disapproval. So even if I had been considering any sort of romance – and, I kept telling myself, that was most definitely not to be entertained, no matter how attractive Mr Roland Newman might be – it would have involved very chaste and very proper behaviour of a sort you really don't see today.

As I look back on my life and the times through which I have lived, I wonder when all this changed. Even the films we went to see at Stamford picture house were scrupulous never to hint at any form of hanky, much less panky. Such kisses as were shown were fleeting or glancing moments and, if ever anyone was depicted in a bedroom, the rules of the day – rigidly enforced by the censor – meant that one foot had to be seen to be firmly rooted to the floor.

They were, I feel comfortable in saying, much more innocent and much less threatening times. And, looking back, I think it was the war, with all its terror and trembling and the need to live for today because the morrow might never come, which swept away the innocence of courting – and, with it, much else of my life and those around me. But I am getting ahead of myself once again. There was one place on the Croome estate where I could be sure no wicked thoughts would intrude. And it was a place that I was required to go every Sunday.

In theory, Sundays were the one day a week I had off (I never quite worked out how Milady managed on those days when my services seemed indispensable every other day of the week) but every member of the household was required to attend church in the morning. Now, as it happened, this was no great burden to me: I loved church and had gone every Sunday back home in Stamford, even though Mum, Dad and my siblings rarely attended services. It wasn't that I was a pious, holier-than-thou Christian: my faith was the quiet sort and very personal to me. No, what I loved best was the singing of hymns and the sense of peace with the world that seemed to imbue me from the moment I stepped across the threshold.

Croome Court, of course, had its own church – the Church of St Mary Magdalene, a neo-gothic building created, inevitably, by Capability Brown with a dominant tower, which was designed to be seen from miles around. Inside, it was a sober and quite small affair with traditional leaded windows and a floor made of stone flags. The three things that struck me immediately on the first day I went there were the pulpit, the pews and the looming presence of dead Coventrys.

The pulpit was a masterwork of intricate wooden carving, set – as with so many churches of the period – up a short set of stone steps to allow the vicar to look down upon his congregation as he (doubtless) chided them for their sins. Croome church also boasted its own priest – not an itinerant parson who held services in a series of churches across the parish. The ordinary pews were nothing special – neither more nor less splendid than in any other church of this size. But what made their arrangement different was the presence of two raised boxes – one on either side – at the back of the church. These were solely for the use of the family and their guests and it rather summed up the whole situation to be looked down on by both my spiritual and temporal betters on my one day a week off.

Then there was the question of Coventrys past to add to the sensation of being observed by Coventrys present. Just about every corner and wall of the church was occupied by the tombs of, or memorials to, previous Earls and Countesses. There were an awful lot of them and their ghostly spirit seemed to fill the church, as if demanding – as the Countess would murmur at breakfast – that God ensure her servants were dutiful and faithful. The latest addition was that of the 9th Earl and Countess: a carefully carved inscription on the wall pronounced that 'they were lovely and pleasant in their lives and in their deaths they were not divided'. Which was, I'm sure, a true and moving sentiment but, as I look back on what was to follow for the 10th Earl and my mistress, I can't escape the feeling that this was both a curse for the living, as well as a blessing on the dead.

Chapter Eight

Huntin', Shootin' – and a Ball

LACK OF SCENT SPOILS SPORT *Worcester Evening News*
The Master was not well enough to hunt the Croome Hounds yesterday, when the mixed pack met at Sheriff's Bench, and Pavitt carried the horn. A biting wind from the north-west made scenting conditions distinctly poor, and hounds could do very little with their first fox from Salford Coppice, and after taking a faint line through the covert and out to the fruit orchards at the top they could not touch it again.

Their second fox from Salford Coppice had broken covert as if for Pitchill, but after running a couple of fields down wind he swung back into the teeth of the gale. Hounds hunted him up to the plough adjoining Commissioner's Coppice, where they came to a check.

Hitting off the line left handed, they skirted the west corner of Salford Coppice and made for the fruit orchards. The fox had evidently turned right-handed from there and made for Norton Hills, but the hounds could make little headway on entering the covert.

After drawing the whole length of Norton Hills, they crossed the road to draw Hipton Hills, from which a fox was quickly away. He ran through Lenchwick Coppice and into Wood Norton, where he promptly got to ground in the drain by the pool and was later accounted for. As hounds were moving away from the drain a holloa was heard near the Rabbit Warrens, and Pavitt quickly slapped hounds on to the line which they hunted nicely left-handed and over the road to the Leason Brakes, where they could only walk on the faintest possible scent, so were stopped and returned to Wood Norton.

They found again before long and hunted through the Ashbeds, above Major Williams and out by Yunnel Hill. Bearing to the left, they ran on by Hipton Hills and over the road to Norton Hills, turning back halfway through this covert and re-crossing the road, to be stopped eventually short of Wood Norton after about an hour's hunting. Hounds hunted well, particularly during the afternoon, though hampered all day by lack of scent.

It's hard to imagine picking up your local newspaper today and finding column after column devoted to the chasing of a fox across miles of countryside – and certainly not in the approving tones that characterise this typical report of the Croome Hunt. But as I settled into life at the Court, hunting – and the regular reporting of it – came to be a dominant feature of my life. The reason was that fox hunting – and, as we'll see, other types of blood sports – were meat and drink to my mistress.

I first heard the sounds one cold and dank day at the start of November. It was the early hours of the morning – no later than 5am and a good two hours before I should have been gently awoken with a cup of tea and a waiting bath – and outside my window it was still pitch black. But through that window I could hear the distant sounds of very excited dogs and the occasional blurt of a horn. The hunting season had started and, without wishing to sound too grumpy about it, my sleep was its first casualty.

I'd been told to expect this the evening before (not that this made my interrupted sleep any better). As I laid out her gown and jewels for dinner, the Countess said, 'I will be riding to hounds tomorrow, Mulley. Please make sure you lay out my clothes this evening: I shall be up with the lark in the morning.'

I quizzed Mr Latter about this downstairs in the

steward's room. I knew, of course, that the gentry liked to occupy themselves with fox hunting but I'd never heard the expression 'riding to hounds' and was distinctly unsure exactly which items of her extensive wardrobe Milady would need preparing. As ever, Mr Latter rode to my rescue.

'Her Ladyship will rise at approximately three o'clock,' he said in his precise and calm way. 'You will not be required to rise at that time and she will bathe when she returns: you must have her bath ready to draw from early afternoon onwards. As to her clothes, she will need her jodhpurs, her chemise, her white stock and her black hunting jacket. Please lay them out in her dressing room while she and His Lordship dine. I will have her riding boots prepared: you do not need to concern yourself with them.'

Well, that all sounded like words from a completely foreign language to me but I made a bee-line for the Countess's wardrobe and carefully explored every possible item of clothing which might correspond to the list Mr Latter had given me. 'Let's hope you've got this right, my girl,' I muttered to myself. 'Her Ladyship is going to be jumping fields and fences tomorrow morning and there's nothing for it but that you have to make sure everything is spit-spot perfect for her when she rises. It wouldn't do for you to fall at this hurdle, so keep your fingers crossed and hope that these are the right togs for chasing foxes.'

I must have somehow managed to lay out the right outfit because Milady didn't summon me at 3am for a dressing-down (or redressing-up). I'm not sure, if she had, what would have happened – I've always enjoyed my sleep and after a day working at the Court I almost fell into bed with tiredness: being snatched from my dreams at such an ungodly hour might well have produced a perilously sharp response! And so Milady rode to hounds and I was woken by their baying and excitement from across the fields.

As with so much else, the Earl and the Countess had their own pack. The Croome Hunt had been founded by the 9th Earl in 1867 and had what it called its own 'country'. This was a territory of about 20 square miles, taking in Worcestershire, Warwickshire and Gloucestershire, over which the hunt had the right to chase foxes. Previously, this land had belonged to the much older Worcestershire Hunt but, in the mysterious way of all things aristocratic, had been carved out and handed over to His Lordship. And what a busy hunt the Croome was. The hunting season began on the first Saturday in November and continued to the following April. In my time at the Court the Croome would set out in pursuit of foxes as often as four days a week and, apparently, it was one of the most successful in the country. *The Complete Foxhunter* – which as far as I know was the closest thing to a bible for the hunting set – describes the territory as 'wonderfully good, there being a fair amount of grass in both Ledbury and Croome domains, while the plough is not particularly deep. Some big woodlands there are, but for all that the bulk of the hunting is in the open, and the Ledbury is, on the whole, a fair scenting country.'

I have to say that fox hunting never held much appeal for me and I can't read something like that without feeling a twinge of sadness and sympathy for the poor beasts chased over hill and dale for the pleasure of the gentry. But then again, I had been brought up in a town and knew nothing of country pursuits and it's fair to say that the Croome Hunt included among its number a goodly proportion of local farmers who presumably had a good reason to get up at 3am and risk life and limb in pursuit of their quarry.

Ever since the 9th Earl founded the Croome, the Coventrys had always been installed as Master of the Hunt. This was no mere honorary position – though it was that too, since it reflected the fact that His Lordship was the biggest single financial contributor to the cost of running it and paid for the upkeep of the pack, as well as employing the staff necessary for maintaining it.

The Croome was quartered at kennels over the fields from the estate in the village of Kinnersley. This was where the packs of hounds lived and where the hunt would gather in the darkness to prepare for their day's sport. Since the crackdown on fox hunting a few years ago, packs like the Croome have been reduced in size and in the number of times they meet. I suppose many people today will never have seen a big hunt gather. Whatever you think about the rights and wrongs – and, as I've said, I have my own views on that – it is a remarkable sight. Oscar Wilde may have called fox hunting 'the unspeakable in full pursuit of the uneatable' but to see those 'unspeakables' in their bright red coats (confusingly called pinks) and the ladies in their smart black coats, their slim necks swaddled in white stocks – well, it's a piece of Old England and even for me it stirs the blood.

You might have noticed at the start of that article from the *Worcester Evening News* that the Master was ill and not able to hunt that morning. As the season wore on, I began to realise that this was a far from unusual occurrence. Whilst my mistress was a dedicated and enthusiastic huntswoman, His Lordship was often 'too ill' to join her and lead the pack.

In the three months I had been in service I had only caught rare glimpses of the Earl. Of course, attending to him was no part of my duties – that was Mr Latter's responsibility as His Lordship's valet (as well as being butler to the house). But I did begin to wonder at how little Lord Coventry was seen. In my conversations, such as they were, with Her Ladyship, I had no doubt that she and her husband were truly in love: theirs was not one of those marriages of convenience or arrangement that the aristocracy so often go in for. But she would occasionally let slip that His Lordship wouldn't be doing this or that – whatever the day held in store for her – because he had taken to his bed. It all seemed a bit mysterious and I resolved to pick up what explanation I could from the snatches of gossip I sometimes heard in the servants' quarters.

Milady returned from hunting in the middle of the afternoon. She was flushed with excitement – if not with success, since a brace of foxes had eluded her and the Croome hounds – and covered from head to toe in mud. She stomped in, still wearing her boots caked with earth and, before I could step forward to greet her, Mr Latter had silently arrived and was helping her remove them. They disappeared together. A few minutes later the Countess emerged clad in her dressing gown.

'I'm ready for my bath now, Mulley,' she said, striding across the floor. 'Please see to it directly.' As I rushed to draw the water and prepare everything she would need, it dawned on me that, to the best of my knowledge, my mistress had not eaten a thing all day, had ridden up to 20 miles and jumped countless stiles and fences. Yet, other than looking a bit like she had been dragged backwards through a hedge, she showed no sign of weariness or fatigue. 'Well, now that just tells you something,' I thought to myself. 'While the master is apparently so poorly that he can't even make it out of bed, Her Ladyship has taken half the county in her stride without so much as a pause. Your mistress is made of strong stuff, my girl, and you'll have your work cut out to keep up.'

While Her Ladyship bathed, I went back down into the servants' quarters in search of Mr Latter. I wasn't sure what was to be done about the Countess's muddy clothes but, since she might very well be needing them again the next day, I was determined to make sure everything was washed, dried and ironed ready, just in case.

I found the butler patiently scraping mud off Milady's riding boots onto an old newspaper. Of her jacket, chemise and stock there was no sign.

'It's all right, Miss Mulley,' he said, sensing my uncertainty. 'I take care of Her Ladyship's boots and her clothes have been taken to the laundry. If you would be so good as to iron them when they return that will be as much as your duties require.'

It only took me one look at the state of the boots and the mud-splattered newspaper to feel rather relieved on that score. If my duties were as limited as this on hunting days, the Countess could ride to hounds every day of the week so far as I was concerned.

Since we're on the subject of duties and newspapers, I'd like to share with you an article published in the *Worcester Evening News* that year. It reported on an apparent trend among servants to demand – and be granted – lavish salaries and a whole heap of luxuries. I have to say that it made my eyes water because nothing in it matched my experiences at Croome Court – and I was pretty certain that, when Dorothy Clark or Mrs Sapstead saw it, they would explode with laughter.

EXCLUSIVE MODEL MAID:
THE MODERN GIRL'S DEMAND

The modern housemaid demands so much in the way of facilities for her pleasure that what some mistresses regard as the model maid seems about as elusive as the scarlet pimpernel. Mistresses broken and shattered in health by the constant worry, seek her here, seek her there, indeed they seek her everywhere, and what a treasure should they find one … 'I am beginning to think that the model maid is as extinct as the Dodo,' lamented a mistress who told an *Evening News* representative that she had tried four servants in less than six months. 'They want all and give little,' she added irritably. Other employers were equally emphatic and some of them declared that they would prefer to do their own housework than be dependent upon maids who left without the slightest provocation.

The head of a large servants registry office consoled with these harassed mistresses. 'Girls will not go into domestic service,' she said, 'unless they are assured of every possible comfort. The position is almost as embarrassing for us as for the mistresses. It is almost impossible to persuade a girl to take a position where she would be lonely. In any case she invariably demands the use of the wireless and gramophone and two or three evenings off a week to go to the pictures.

There is a parlour-maid employed near Hampstead Heath who owns her own house and goes riding on the heath at least once each day.

'Maids have even been known to ride in Rotten Row,' an employer told the reporter. The Duchess of Atholl once suggested that mistresses did not give sufficient thought to providing servants with prettily decorated bedrooms or offer sufficient facilities for indoor and outdoor recreation. 'We have even gone to that length,' was the comment of a mistress. One employer said she had discovered the secret of keeping her maid. 'I allow Phyllis to entertain her young man in the kitchen when she is not off-duty.'

I have to say I'd never read such rubbish in my life. Three evenings off per week? Going riding in Rotten Row (which I'd never heard of but turned out to be a famous pathway in London's Hyde Park)? And owning a house? Good grief, if this was the life some servants were living, I can assure you it wasn't what we were used to at Croome. And as for ladies being 'broken and shattered in health' – well, from what I'd just seen, my mistress was as healthy as a horse and probably a great deal less shattered than the one she'd just ridden for a full day. No, the newspaper was not to be relied on, I decided.

As it happened, I was closer to the truth than I knew. For that year trouble was brewing – trouble which would eventually turn the country on its head, despite the best efforts of newspapers to keep it all under wraps. It began in December with word that the King's health was declining. His Majesty had been seriously ill for many years, the result, largely, of his habit of chain smoking cigarettes. But 1935 was the silver jubilee of his accession to the throne and, in a way that I don't think people understand today, he was both a distant and severe father figure to the nation and, at the same time, genuinely loved.

So news of his latest illness was received with solemnity and sadness. In the servants' quarters at Croome it was discussed in hushed voices, as if our chatter could somehow disturb the King in his bed more than a hundred miles away at Windsor. It cast a shadow over the growing excitement of the season.

Christmas was coming and what a sense of excitement began to take over the Court. Deliveries of food and drink began arriving almost daily, keeping Winnie busy in her pantry, while in his room Mr Latter set to, to write down all the fine wines, ports and brandies in the large ledger he kept as the necessary records of what was in the vast cellar full of alcoholic drinks. The Earl and the Countess were never great entertainers but, as the month wore on, so did the frequency of their dinner parties increase. These were grand affairs and Winnie would hardly know if she was coming or going, what with making all the courses – and there were several on each occasion – from scratch. I, of course, had little part in the proceedings but for the poor kitchen and scullery maid it was a time of constant scrubbing of vegetables and beating of eggs, while the ovens positively groaned with freshly baked bread and whatever fish, fowl or flesh was on the menu. But if I was, by dint of my position, somewhat apart from all that was going on, the Coventrys' dinner parties did bring me two very welcome benefits.

The first was that Winnie put aside the leftovers (and some which might not strictly ever have seen the tables upstairs!) and we head servants had first go at them. In truth, this was something of a double treat since, not only were we dining on very fine fare indeed but, when it came to our normal below-stairs meals, Winnie was not what you could call the most careful of cooks. Many was the time in that year – and those which followed – when a row would break out in the kitchen over the vittals we were served up. It would typically start with a sigh from Mr Latter and a regretful expression as to the delights of our dinner. 'Winnie, Winnie – what have you done to this?' would be his normal opening remark, to be followed by a generally good-natured – though undoubtedly pointed – ribbing over something that was overdone, or underdone or just plain not there at all. Now, Winnie Sapstead was, in many ways, quite highly strung and it wouldn't take long before her dander was up and she and Mr Latter would be going at it hammer and tongs – and (at least figuratively) soup ladles and saucepans as well. But give Winnie her due, the dinners she and her staff prepared for the gentry – well, they were a fine sight to see and a delight to taste. And so when we got to sup from their menus, it was very welcome indeed.

The other benefit which came my way walked into the servants' quarters on the first fancy dinner party that December. Roland Newman had put aside his chauffeuring and waterworks duties to come and help out as an assistant footman. He was quickly put to work by Mr Latter, whose job it was to make sure that the servants waiting on the groaning tables upstairs did so almost without being noticed. But I noticed him, and he noticed me, and both of us were pleased to do so.

Christmas wasn't just about the increased pace of life upstairs: it meant a little something coming our way below them too – and also the highlight of the year for people in service: the Servants' Ball.

In those days every great house had a Servants' Ball – though not, for reasons you'll see, all at the same time of year. In the grandest of them all – places such as Welbeck Abbey, where the Duke of Portland employed more than 60 staff in the house, with a further 200 labouring away in the stables, gardens and home farm – the Ball would be an incredibly lavish affair, more grand even than many of those held by royalty today. For example, Welbeck's annual Servants' Ball was so huge and so posh that the Duke paid for an orchestra and 50 waiters to be brought in from London.

At Croome – and this was possibly another sign of the money worries that were bearing down on His Lordship – the Earl didn't go in for anything so expensive. The music was to be provided by a gramophone and, as for servants, well, we all mucked in to serve the food ourselves. But the food was good (although no alcohol was permitted) and there was to be dancing.

'Her Ladyship will open the dancing by taking a turn round the floor with me,' Mr Latter told me as the great day drew near. I looked at the floor of the servants' hall and wondered if its rough and uneven flagstones might not catch Milady's dainty slippers and the whole evening would come crashing down. But evidently nothing like this had ever happened and Mr Latter moved on to my role in the proceedings.

'After that His Lordship will approach you and ask you for the second dance. You are, of course, to accept graciously.' Well, I don't know about being gracious but I certainly knew my place – and in any case, I couldn't resist a little thrill at the prospect: here I was, Hilda Mulley, just a slip of a girl from a very humble background and, within a few months of leaving Stamford, I would be dancing cheek to cheek with one of the oldest and most noble aristocrats in the land. That was something to write home about, to be sure.

But that thought also brought a little sadness to my mind. I would have to write and tell Mum and Dad that for the first time ever I wouldn't be with them at Christmas. One of the prices paid for being in service was that work didn't stop for the season: the Croome Court would still need to be kept running. For all of us below stairs, that meant that work didn't stop as it might if you were working in a factory or in an office. Christmas Day was the one day off we were given – and even then all of the staff were required to attend the morning service in Croome church. The knowledge that I wouldn't see Mum and Dad, or Joan and Jim, at Christmas took a bit of the edge of my excitement.

When Christmas Eve came – the night of the Servants' Ball – what a hustle and bustle there was throughout the house. Our routine duties continued as normal: I brought the Countess her cup of tea, ran her bath and laid out her clothes just like any normal day and, for Winnie, the work was, if anything, even more demanding than usual. But I think I detected in my mistress's rich strong voice – which now I had come to know it, had a tinge of a lovely Welsh accent to it – a little less formality and a little more warmth.

For my part, I was anxious to get ready for the evening. I had made myself a new dress for the occasion – a lovely long gown in my favourite dark green and trimmed with white 'fur' (of course, it wasn't real fur – I couldn't afford that on five bob a week) and I needed to make the final adjustments to it.

The evening was set to start at 6pm and by late afternoon I was freed from my duties in time to put the finishing touches to my dress. Winnie and Mr Latter knew I had been hard at work on it for several weeks and one or other of them produced a camera – a little old Box Brownie, which, if you've never seen one, was really no more than a cardboard box and a tiny lens. To my absolute astonishment, they told me I was to go and put on my new gown and make my way up to the very top of the Court and then out onto the rooftop. There was a sort of a walkway up there between the roof tiles and the ornamental topping and I was to meet them up there.

I scurried along the basement corridor and flew up the great stone staircase – I made a mental note that, if I wasn't careful one day, I would come a cropper on the slippery steps – until I gained the sanctuary of my room. Here, with my fingers all a-fumble, I somehow managed to get into my gown and, after flapping and fussing with the trim, I climbed the steep staircase to the roof and stepped out onto what seemed to me like the battlements of some great castle.

Mr Latter and Winnie were waiting for me and for the first time in my adult life I was told to pose for the camera. Looking at the picture now, I can see a grin on my face that stretches from ear to ear. Fancy little old me having their portrait taken on the very roof of such a great house. By the time I clambered my way back down to the servants' quarters I must have looked like the Cheshire Cat!

At 6pm sharp my mistress swept into the big room where our ball was to be held. But of the Earl there was no sign.

'His Lordship is indisposed and I am afraid he will not be able to join you all tonight,' the Countess announced. Hmm, there it was again, that slight sense of something not being quite right. The Earl was quite a young man in those days – just 35 years of age, which was younger than Mr

Latter and, indeed, Winnie. Could he really be so poorly as not to be able to spend just a few minutes with his servants on Christmas Eve?

'Well,' I thought to myself as the Countess took to the floor for the first dance with Mr Latter, 'at least I shall be spared the embarrassment of having to step out with His Lordship this evening.' Much as I loved dancing, I had been quietly dreading the moment when I would have to join hands with an aristocrat and, for all I knew, one or other of us was quite likely to turn the whole business into a ridiculous spectacle. 'It's an ill wind that doesn't blow some good, at least,' I thought.

My mistress didn't stay long with us that evening but before she left she handed out Christmas gifts to all the staff. I think for most of them she placed a small brown envelope with a few silver coins in their outstretched hands. But for me she had something special: it was a beautiful brooch, which sparkled and shone as if the stones in it were real diamonds. I wasn't so silly as to think that they would be real but, to me, it was the most precious thing I had ever owned and I pinned it on my new gown with pride and with a promise that I should never, ever let it go.

I couldn't have known how, in a few short years, that promise would be betrayed and all the happiness and warmth that I felt that night would be snatched away from me.

Chapter Nine

The Abdication

On the evening of Monday, 20 January 1936, all of us in service at Croome Court were sitting quietly in the hall where the under servants took their meals. We were clustered around a big, old-fashioned wireless set, staring at its lacquered woodwork and glowing valves. We were waiting for an announcement from London.

From 9.30pm onwards the ordinary broadcasting programmes were stopped and all the stations of the BBC, including those conducting the shortwave service transmitted to Britain's far-flung Empire, were linked together but kept utterly silent, save for the transmission of an official bulletin at 15-minute intervals. The subject of that bulletin was the rapidly deteriorating medical condition of His Majesty, King George V. At 10pm, as we sat there in hushed respect, a short service of recollection and prayer for the King was broadcast, after which the silent watch between bulletins was resumed.

Finally, at a little after midnight, the tired, upper-class voice of a BBC announcer crackled across the airwaves: 'This is London. The following bulletin was issued at nine-twenty-five. The King's life is moving peacefully towards its close.'

It is hard for me to put into words how deeply sad we ordinary people felt that night. In those long-ago days the King was as central to our lives as anything you can imagine. Our loyalty to him was something we imbibed with our mothers' milk and was as taken for granted as the mugs of strong brown tea that sustained the nation.

Yet it is also true to say that we knew almost nothing of him and little of his family. Indeed, I don't think I ever heard the phrase 'the Royal Family' in all of my time in service – that was a much later creation and one which arrived hand in hand with the demystifying of our monarchy through the medium of television. In that first month of 1936 I doubt you could have found anyone of our class who would know the names of any but the closest of the King's family; but by the same token, I'm sure you would have to search long and hard to find any man, woman or child who would hear a word said against him. If he was a distant father figure, well, then he was still the nation's father: that's how we felt back then.

Although the idea of television had been invented by then (news of a proposal 12 months earlier to begin work on a broadcasting network had been given a cautious welcome by the *Worcester Evening Post* and had been much discussed below stairs at Croome), the wireless was our main source of contact with the outside world. In fact, for all of us there on that sad night, there was a strange sense of community with the rest of Britain and her still-mighty Empire. The BBC Home Service (as it was then called) was like a gigantic public-address system, with literally millions of listeners in all parts of the world all tuning in at the same time, hanging on every last word about the deteriorating health – and ultimate quiet passing – of their Sovereign.

'We will stand for a minute of silence,' instructed Mr Latter. And we all got to our feet, our heads bowed and deep in our own thoughts, as 60 seconds of silent respect were observed.

I suppose there must have been the same tableau played out in homes up and down the land – from terraced cottages like the one where my parents stood, heads bowed, to the greatest of houses occupied by the gentry and their staff. But in many of those – as in ours – the passing of the King had a significance that did not apply to the ordinary people of Britain. There would be a coronation, and our masters and mistresses must play their parts in its pomp and pageantry.

First, there was to be a funeral and the question of the succession. On Tuesday, 28 January the streets of London were lined with people as, under grey and rain-filled skies, at 9.45am the King's coffin was placed upon a gun carriage to be escorted by an honour guard of his soldiers to its final resting place. In those pre-television days none of us could watch the procession – at least, not as it happened. But the cameras of Pathé Newsreel were present and within days a special ten-minute film was playing in cinemas the length and breadth of Britain. The grainy film and cloudy skies were made even more sombre by the near complete silence. The Queen was captured, clad from head to toe in black widow's weeds, climbing into the State carriage. The narrator's voice on the film solemnly announced that the world was watching.

It has been the Empire taking leave of its beloved father … and the world takes leave of the man who was the symbol of all the might, majesty and power of the British Commonwealth of Nations.

The procession, led by the King's son, included five kings of European countries: one of the last times – had we but known it – that there would be so many monarchs gathered together in one place. This, I felt, was more than the passing of our dear King: it was the end of an era – and who could know what the next one would bring. There had already been one unpromising sign: during the procession, part of the Imperial State Crown had fallen from on top of the coffin and landed in the gutter as the cortège turned into New Palace Yard. The new King, Edward VIII, saw it fall and, so we were told, wondered whether it was a bad omen for his coming reign.

It's one of the funny things about the aristocracy that they don't seem to be in any hurry to get things done. And so Edward's coronation was set to take place more than a full year after he technically ascended to the throne, in May 1937. From my point of view, though, this would be a good thing: Mr Latter had already told all of the Croome servants that the Earl and the Countess would be among the first names on the guest list – and that meant an enormous amount of extra work for the whole household.

In the meantime, though, 1936 had only just started and the year stretched out before us. Milady still went fox hunting (while His Lordship seemed to cry off as many times as possible); their children were growing and becoming quite a handful; and as February turned to March, one morning the Countess had new instructions for me.

'We are to go away from Croome, Mulley. We are to spend a week or so at Amroth. Please see to it that all I will need is packed carefully and made ready.'

'Of course, Milady. Will His Lordship be coming – and

the children too?' I could have guessed the answer but I asked the question nonetheless.

'No, Mulley. His Lordship will be staying here at Croome. As for the children, Lady Joan and Lady Maria will be away at school but the younger two will be coming with us.'

'How shall we travel there, Milady? Isn't Amroth a long way from here?'

'Roland will drive us in the Standard,' she said – and my heart skipped a little beat. 'Steady, girl,' I told myself. 'Just you steady down now.'

Amroth – or to use its full title, Amroth Castle – was, indeed, a fair old haul. It was the family seat of Her Ladyship's mother and father, Lord and Lady Kylsant, more than 160 miles away near Carmarthen on the South Wales coast. It was the first time that my mistress had returned home – at least in the time I'd been with her – since her father had been released from his 12-month jail sentence for fraud. I have to say that I was very glad my Mum and Dad didn't know about the visit: I could just imagine Dad's reaction – 'My girl in the house of a jailbird!' – and hear the sound of his foot being put down very firmly indeed.

As it was, I knew next to nothing about Lord and Lady Kylsant, nor about the kind of household and servant staff they kept after his fall into disgrace. But my mistress was about to fill in at least one gap in my knowledge and, with it, dash any hopes I might have had of the possibility of seeing the dapper chauffeur about the castle.

'Robert will be staying in an hotel in Carmarthen, Mulley. Lady Kylsant is very strict about propriety and it wouldn't do for a male servant to be seen staying in the same house as one of our female staff.'

'Well,' I thought, 'it's perfectly all right for you to go and stay in the house of a man who has brought dishonour on your family name – and to drag me there with you – but when it comes to us servants, we must be seen to curtsey and bow in the face of what's proper. Father or no father, I know what that smells like.' But I kept this thought to myself. No good would come of upsetting the apple cart – even if I'd ever thought of speaking back to Milady. 'Anyway,' I told myself, 'you just jolly well stop those silly girlish thoughts of romance. They're a short cut to a very swift downfall and an aristocratic boot propelling you out the door.' Still, the double standards – for that's what they were – rankled with me and I wasn't looking forward to the visit, not one bit.

I'd like to be able to tell you that I was proved wrong; that our stay in Amroth Castle was as pleasant an experience as it could be for a lady's maid. But I can't. The journey was very long – not only did cars travel a lot more slowly in those days but the roads themselves were nothing like as solid and reliable as they are today – and no one had even heard the word motorway. It took hours and hours to get there and, once we arrived, I found Lord and Lady Kylsant's staff to be stand-offish and not at all friendly. 'Well, maybe there's a reason for that,' I told myself. After all, it's the gentry that set the tone and the standards, and that didn't exactly look promising when you thought about the recent past. All in all, I was glad to get back to Croome – and that's something I hadn't thought I'd hear myself thinking.

Back in the relative comfort of the servants' quarters – and of my enormous bedroom, which, I'm slightly ashamed to say, I had begun to take for granted – I made two distinct resolutions. The first was to find out a little bit more about His Lordship and why he so rarely accompanied my mistress. The second was to allow myself the chance to consider a romance. Although Roland Newman had been forced to sleep in the dubious comfort of a Carmarthen hotel, I'd seen enough of him to realise that I was beginning to have feelings for him.

As I write this, I'm smiling at those words – 'beginning to have feelings': what a terribly old-fashioned and quaint way of putting it! These days I'm sure girls of my age – and remember, I was only just 20 – would say something like 'I had begun to fancy him' or 'he was a bit of all right'. But none of those words would have ever entered my head. No, the 1930s were very much more genteel about matters of the heart, even for servants such as us.

In the end, the first resolution proved more difficult than

the second. Mr Latter was a tartar when it came to gossiping about the family. If he ever caught the lower servants doing it, he'd give them a right royal dressing-down.

'The Earl and the Countess put their trust in us and we are grateful to them for doing so. We must never – ever – spread tittle-tattle or rumours about our family. They are our betters and our masters and, whatever may (or may not) happen in their lives, it is simply not our place to have an opinion about it, much less to discuss these worthless thoughts with anyone else.'

Well, that told all of us! And for all that we knew that Mr Latter was a good and kind man – in a way he was like a father figure to the younger staff like me – I don't think any of us doubted that a first offence of gossiping would be bad, but a second would mean the sack.

So it proved very difficult to discover anything very much about the 10th Earl of Coventry. Other than Mr Latter, he very rarely saw any of the staff and it wasn't just hunting that he avoided with his own class. I came to notice that, often as not, when Milady told me to prepare her evening wear and her best jewels for a dinner out at some other aristocrat's house, His Lordship would be unwell and unable to go. On many of those occasions the Countess would be accompanied – because it wasn't seemly for a titled Lady to arrive on her own for a dinner – by His Lordship's brother, John.

Now, I don't want you to get carried away. I know what this might look like to modern eyes but, as I keep trying to remind you, this was the 1930s and, as far as I knew, there was nothing more to this arrangement than the Earl's brother acting as a chaperone. I was – and I remain – convinced that my mistress truly loved the Earl and, in any event, there had been quite enough scandal in the family without any of that sort of business.

My other resolution proved a little easier. It started with a message from Roland's mother: would I like to come to lunch on my day off at their little cottage in Severn Stoke? Would I? I should think so! It was arranged that after I'd been to church the following Sunday I would spruce myself up – I wanted to make an impression, not just on Roland but on his parents. The invitation was couched in terms of simply being kind – a young girl, miles away from her family and stuck out in the vastness of Croome was bound to be a bit lonely and perhaps a bit at a loose end. But I knew that beneath that innocent cover there might well be the first hints of romance. I didn't think that Roland had ever asked anyone else from the Court home to meet his parents – and in those days that sort of invitation was the very chaste first step on the way to asking a girl out.

But there was one little problem to be solved: how would I get to Severn Stoke? The village was a few miles away from Croome and it would take several hours to walk there after church. Now, you might think that this wouldn't be an issue: after all, Roland was a chauffeur and in charge of the Coventry's cars. Surely he would be able to pick me up in the blue hound van, if nothing else. But this was where His Lordship's generous treatment of his servants stopped: Roland was forbidden to use any of the vehicles except on official family business.

The solution, when it turned up that Sunday morning, was noisy and almost as smelly as the hound van. I looked out of my bedroom window to see a motorbike put-putting towards the Court and a figure almost swamped by an enormous leather coat sat on top of it. This was to be my transport to Severn Stoke and I don't mind admitting that my heart sank a little. Not only because I'd never sat on a motorbike before but because it was almost guaranteed to ruin my efforts at looking my best to meet his parents. I sighed inwardly and resigned myself to landing there looking like I'd been out on one of my mistress's fox-hunting jaunts. Which is just how it turned out to be.

Luckily, Roland's parents were sensible, down-to-earth sort of people with no airs or graces, and the Sunday lunch passed off easily and happily. In fact, when it was time to go back, I felt a pang of sadness at having to leave their cosy little cottage, which reminded me of my parents' house in Stamford, to return to the cold grandness of Croome Court. I had then the sense once again of going back to prison – a magnificent and (even for us servants) luxurious one to be sure, but a prison nonetheless. I remembered one of the songs that Dad had learned in his childhood and would occasionally sing when the Mulley family got together round the piano.

> She's just a bird in a gilded cage
> A beautiful sight to see
> You may think she's happy and free from care
> She's not, though she seems to be …

'Well, amen to that,' I said to myself that Sunday, as I clung to Roland's leather coat and his little motorcycle chugged and tugged me back to the Court. But I climbed the stairs to my bedroom with a warm feeling inside nonetheless: Roland's parents had insisted I go to lunch again the following week.

Just as my love life, with all its sweet scents of secrecy (don't forget, the merest hint of a romance could have got both Roland and I the boot, no questions asked), was looking a little brighter, the dangers of another illicit and unsanctioned love affair were about to be starkly revealed. When they did, the whole of Britain – and, above all, the aristocracy – was to be thrown into chaos and consternation.

King Edward – for that's what he was styled, even though there had as yet been no coronation – was a bachelor but for the previous few years he had often been accompanied at private social events by Wallis Simpson, the American wife of rich British shipping executive Ernest Simpson. He was Wallis's second husband; her first marriage had ended in divorce in 1927 and, in and of itself, it was quite shocking for Edward to be seen in the company of a divorced woman – doubly so when she was still the wife of another man. But Edward seemed able and willing to ignore all the social conventions that governed the lives of his subjects and, throughout 1936, Wallis Simpson attended more official functions as the King's guest. These were announced in the Court Circular in *The Times* every morning and it was noticeable that, although her name appeared regularly, the name of her husband was conspicuously absent. Tongues began to wag in aristocratic circles and, inevitably, some of the gossip leaked down to their servants. I don't think we at Croome ever learned of the growing scandal from the Earl or the Countess but servants from other great houses sometimes stayed at the Court when their masters and mistresses came to weekend parties – and, by the same token, we often stayed at other grand mansions belonging to the gentry.

In the summer of 1936 the King should have gone to spend the traditional royal retreat at Balmoral. But in a sudden and shocking breach of protocol, he refused and chose instead to holiday with Mrs Simpson in the eastern

Mediterranean on board the steam yacht *Nahlin*. The government – and especially the Prime Minister of the day, Stanley Baldwin – was appalled and tried to reason with Edward but he remained stubborn and resolute.

Now, if the King's subjects had known all of this, I don't doubt we would have been as dismayed as Mr Baldwin. For a start, there was a very great distrust of anything foreign – and especially of anything to do with what ordinary people still called 'the Continong'. For our nation's father to be cavorting on a yacht there was bad enough but to do so with a divorcee who was still married: well, it would have seemed like the rules by which we had to live just didn't apply to the gentry.

But we didn't know – not for a while at least. Do you remember I said that the newspapers didn't always tell us the truth in those days? In truth, they were sometimes no more than the mouthpiece for the rich and powerful. It was easy enough for Mr Baldwin and his government to persuade them to keep any mention of the King's indiscretions out of the papers.

The cruise was, however, widely covered in the American and continental European press, and expatriate Britons, who had access to the foreign reports, were scandalised by the reports. They sent letters home to families back in Britain and soon enough the country was talking about little else. By October it was rumoured in high society – and because

he is aware of his need. Some of us wish that he gave more positive signs of his awareness.' And at that point all hell broke loose. The press took the bishop's speech as a deliberate public comment by an important figure on the crisis, and the King's love life became front-page news the following day. It was even reported on the wireless, which told us – since the BBC was usually completely deferential – there was going to be big trouble.

Maybe it's difficult in these more open – some would say more enlightened – days to understand how much this meant to us and how shocking people like me found the King's behaviour. I suppose the nearest most of you have come to anything like it was the whole sorry saga of Prince Charles and Lady Diana. But in 1936 people felt the crisis much more deeply. The King was still seen as the father of the country – a wise and steady hand on the tiller of the ship of State. And there was, too, a sense that for him to live by different standards than was expected of his subjects was to undermine the whole structure of the nation. As for me – well, I had a very personal axe to grind about the whole affair. I was having to keep secret my growing love for Roland – who was a perfectly respectable bachelor with no skeletons in his closet – for fear of losing my position. 'Sauce for the goose should be sauce for the gander,' I muttered to myself as news of the King's dallying with the unquestionably 'fast' Mrs Simpson gripped Britain.

Day after day the crisis got worse. Acting on the advice of Edward's staff, Mrs Simpson decided to escape from the intense press and public attention and left Britain for the south of France on 3 December. At a tearful farewell, the King told her, 'I shall never give you up.'

A week later came the news the whole country had been dreading. Edward had decided to step down from the throne – to abdicate. Nothing like this had ever happened in the whole history of the British monarchy and, for ordinary people like us below stairs at Croome, the word 'abdicate' was completely unknown: we had to look it up in a dictionary. I can't properly describe the feelings of shock and fear that gripped us. It was as if the whole, well-ordered world we had known was coming to an end.

On Friday, 11 December 1936 we clustered round the wireless set in the servants' hall. The BBC had announced that the King was to make an address to his people. But as we sat in tense silence, the stern, Scottish voice of the BBC's Director General introduced him not as our King but as His Royal Highness, Prince Edward. And then came the speech that marked the beginning of the end.

At long last I am able to say a few words of my own. I have never wanted to withhold anything, but until now it has not been constitutionally possible for me to speak. A few hours ago I discharged my last duty as King and Emperor, and now that I have been succeeded by my brother, the Duke of York, my first words must be to declare my allegiance to him. This I do with all my heart.

You all know the reasons which have impelled me to renounce the throne. But I want you to understand that in making up my mind I did not forget the country or the empire, which, as Prince of Wales and lately as King, I have for twenty-five years tried to serve. But you must believe me when I tell you that I have found it impossible to carry the heavy burden of responsibility and to discharge my duties as King as I would wish to do without the help and support of the woman I love.

As Edward's rich, plummy voice echoed round the servants' hall, I looked across at Mr Latter. His face was a mask, showing no emotion – though I know, like all of us, he must have been churning inside. 'Here,' I thought, 'is how we are meant to behave; here are the standards which we are expected to keep up.' It wouldn't do for poor Mr Latter to show any emotion: he was expected to keep a stiff upper lip and to keep all us servants calm and respectful. I looked round at the honest, fearful faces of ordinary people as Edward's voice carried on.

And I want you to know that the decision I have made has been mine and mine alone. This was a thing I had to judge entirely for myself. The other person most nearly concerned has tried up to the last to persuade me to take a different course. I have made this, the most serious decision of my life, only upon the single thought of what would, in the end, be best for all.

This decision has been made less difficult to me by the sure knowledge that my brother, with his long training in the public affairs of this country and with his fine qualities, will be able to take my place forthwith without interruption or injury to the life and progress of the empire. And he has one matchless blessing, enjoyed by so many of you, and not bestowed on me – a happy home with his wife and children.

During these hard days I have been comforted by Her Majesty my mother and by my family. The ministers of the crown, and in particular, Mr. Baldwin, the Prime Minister, have always treated me with full consideration. There has never been any constitutional difference between me and them, and between me and Parliament. Bred in the constitutional tradition by my father, I should never have allowed any such issue to arise.

Ever since I was Prince of Wales, and later on when I occupied the throne, I have been treated with the greatest kindness by all classes of the people wherever I have lived or journeyed throughout the empire. For that I am very grateful.

I now quit altogether public affairs and I lay down my burden. It may be some time before I return to my native land, but I shall always follow the fortunes of the British race and empire with profound interest, and if at any time in the future I can be found of service to his majesty in a private station, I shall not fail.

And now, we all have a new King. I wish him and you, his people, happiness and prosperity with all my heart. God bless you all! God save the King!

Mr Latter stood up and switched off the wireless set. With a grim face he told us to stand up. 'God save the King,' he said quietly. 'God save the King,' we chorused – though which King each of us was thinking of was anyone's guess.

Chapter Ten

The Year of Accidents –
and the Coronation

I don't know if it was the abdication, coming right at the end of a year in which we had already lost one King, but 1937 seemed to be a year blighted by accidents.

They began on the great stone steps leading from the servants' quarters to the top of the house: the very staircase I had already warned myself to beware of because of the shiny slipperiness of many of the steps. These stairs had already been the scene of a reprimand from Her Ladyship. She had called down for me one day – I don't know why she didn't just ring the bell with my name on it, installed on a board of similar bells at the foot of the stairs. As I hurried to heed my mistress's voice, I had called up, 'Coming, Your Ladyship,' only to be greeted with a sharp reprimand from the Countess when I reached her rooms

'How many times must I tell you, Mulley? You address me as Milady – never, ever as Your Ladyship. Do you understand?'

Well, of course I understood. I'd been very careful always to mind my Ps and Qs and to be sure to use the correct form of address when speaking to the gentry. I had only rarely forgotten – once I referred to my mistress in front of another fine lady as Lady Coventry and suffered the mortifying indignity of being corrected publicly: 'Mulley, I am the Countess of Coventry, not Lady Coventry. Do try to remember, please.' And there I was again getting ticked off for using the wrong term, in my rush to do her bidding. There was a small part of me that felt it shouldn't really matter – but the rest of me very sensibly shut that part up. 'I'm very sorry, Milady. It won't happen again.' And I made sure it didn't.

With that history, I suppose I shouldn't have been surprised when the great staircase was the cause of a rather nasty accident. I had been about my duties, pressing my mistress's clothes or sewing on some buttons in my bedroom, when I was summoned to her presence. There was no question of finishing what I was doing – Her Ladyship insisted on being attended promptly – and so I quickly put down my work and ran to the stairs. As I reached the banister at the very top, the heel of my shoe caught on something – I never knew what but probably it was the edge of the step – and I flew head over heels down flight after flight. I was going so fast that I ended up right at the very bottom of the house, in the servants' corridor, my legs tangled up behind me and my body twisted into goodness knows what position. It felt like every bone in my body had been snapped in two and then rudely shoved into places where they weren't meant to be. I howled with pain.

'Mulley!' Through a fog of pain I heard Milady's voice calling to me down the stairs. 'Mulley, what has happened? Why are you making that noise?' I really didn't have it in me to reply: even if all my bones weren't screaming beneath my skin, the fall had knocked the breath out of me. Luckily for me, Winnie Sapstead came running along the corridor from the kitchen and took charge.

'Miss Mulley's had a fall, Milady. I think she's quite badly hurt!'

Mr Latter and some of the other servants rushed to where I was still whimpering with pain. As Winnie carefully ran her fingers over me, trying to discover whether I had actually broken anything, or at least anything serious, I saw the Countess's feet and legs appear on the stairs above me and very shortly my mistress was standing beside me.

'What have you done, Mulley? How on earth did this happen?' I opened my mouth to try and explain but Mr Latter cut in quickly.

'I believe Miss Mulley has fallen down the stairs, Milady. Quite possibly from the very top of the house. I think, perhaps, we should send for doctor.'

Sending for the doctor was a big thing. This was a long time before the National Health Service was even thought of, much less brought in, and doctor's charged a pretty penny to pay a visit to a patient's home. What's more, they made good and sure they got paid there and then. It crossed my mind as to how I was going to pay him: five bob a week didn't go a long way towards the price of a medical man.

Of course, I needn't have worried. One of the benefits – unspoken ones, for no one ever mentioned this to me when I got the job – of being in service was that the family you worked for paid for the doctor when illness or injury stopped you doing your job. As Mr Latter shooed the other staff away, Winnie whispered to me that it would be all right and that the servants' doctor was going to be telephoned right away. That was the other thing about being in service: those below stairs were never treated by the same doctor as the gentry themselves.

But then my mistress did something completely out of the ordinary. 'Mr Latter,' she said calmly. 'Please ensure you telephone my personal doctor. I should like him to examine Miss Mulley, not your usual one.' Well, the look on Mr Latter's face would have been a picture, I'm sure. I wasn't in any condition to twist my head round to look but he must have been as astonished as I was. For a servant to be treated by Her Ladyship's personal physician was something completely unheard of. What on earth could it mean?

'Very good, Milady,' I heard him say before he walked briskly to the telephone set on a table outside his room. It was one of the old-fashioned types, which you see in films, and I could hear him lift up the old black Bakelite earpiece and then turn the dial to telephone the doctor.

'Thank you, Milady,' I managed to stammer. 'And I'm truly sorry to have caused such a fuss. I'm sure I'll be right as ninepence in no time.'

If I was expecting the Countess to continue with the concern that she had showed by sending for her own doctor, I was brought up short.

'Yes, well, Mulley,' she said abruptly, 'how did this come to occur? What was it that caused you to fall down the stairs?'

'I think I must have caught my heel on the top step, Milady. I felt it catch and really that's the last thing I remember about it until I found myself here at the bottom of the stairs.'

The Countess stepped around me and examined my shoes. She stood up and spoke quite sternly – there was no trace of sympathy now in her voice.

'How many times have I told you not to wear shoes with such a high heel, Mulley? If I've said it once, I have said it a hundred times. Those heels are much too high and the shoes are completely unsuitable. Please ensure you do not wear them again.'

And with that, she turned and was back off up the stairs to her quarters. 'Well,' I thought to myself, 'that's you told good and proper, Hilda Mulley. So much for Lady Bountiful and the fancy doctor: when it comes down to it, you're going to be bossed about even when you've fallen down three flights of stairs and damn near broken your neck!'

But of one thing I was certain: whatever Milady said, I wasn't about to stop wearing those shoes because they had high heels for a very good reason. I was no more than 5 feet tall and my mistress a good 12 inches taller. If I didn't have some kind of heel on my shoes, I should spend all my days with my head at the level of her aristocratic bosom – and, whilst there were many things I was prepared to put up with, that was quite definitely not one of them.

As luck would have it, I hadn't broken any bones, although the doctor did insist on several days of rest with no duties. I felt a bit of a fraud sitting there in my bedroom or in the steward's room and I felt a bit guilty that, on top of her other duties, poor Dorothy Clark was once again having to spend an hour every morning brushing Her Ladyship's hair as well as all the other tasks a ladies' maid was required to perform.

It wasn't too many weeks before the next accident dropped on us at the Court, and this time the roles were reversed from that day when I fell down the stairs. The Countess had gone off on one of her early-morning expeditions with the Croome Hunt. His Lordship had, once again, been too unwell to accompany her. I was preparing her clothes, ready for her return, when I heard a commotion down in the servants' quarters and the sound of Mr Latter once again using the telephone. Not thinking too much about it, I carried on with my task, until Dorothy came and found me, her face white with shock and worry

'Her Ladyship has had an accident while riding to hounds,' she said in a shaky voice. 'It looks to be rather a bad fall and she's to be brought here so that the doctor can examine her.'

Now, riding falls can be very dangerous and I knew from talk amongst the servants that Milady was an adventurous and daring rider. If there was a fox to be had, she was leading the charge at full gallop and, if there were hedges or stiles to be jumped, she barely slowed her horse before leaping them and tearing back into the chase. With Mr Latter's permission, I went upstairs to the great entrance hall and stood beside him, ready for the moment when the Countess was brought in. As we waited, I noticed there were two deep indentations in the stone floor, exactly where his feet were set – grooves worn down by generations of butlers waiting for the gentry.

My mistress's face was drip-white when she was carried in through the door. Her clothes were torn and muddy and she was plainly in a great deal of pain. I expected her to call for her husband whilst she waited for the doctor to attend her. But instead, she said a quite extraordinary thing:

'I want Mulley to look after me. No one else. You may all go about your duties. Mulley shall be my nurse and attendant.'

You could have knocked me down with the proverbial feather! I wasn't even 21 – which made me legally still a child – and I'd never really got a sense from the Countess that I was any more than a servant to her. But here she was, in a great deal of pain and distress, and I was the only one she wanted near her. I must have made some kind of human impression for, when anyone is badly hurt, I guarantee that the person they want to look after them is a person they feel very close to.

Her Ladyship was laid up for some weeks after her fall. I brought her meals to her boudoir and did my best to ensure that she had everything she could want. But the thing she really wanted was to be up in the saddle again and out chasing foxes across the Worcestershire countryside – and that was not about to happen quickly. In the end, I'm not sure if she did ride to hounds again that season – which is probably a good thing, since the greatest occasion for many a long year was approaching.

The new King – George VI – was to be crowned on the day originally planned for Edward's coronation: Wednesday, 12 May 1937. And the Earl and the Countess were among the gentry invited to be part of the ceremony in Westminster Abbey.

The servants' quarters at Croome Court were positively bustling with excitement. After the shocking events of the previous year and the national condemnation of Edward for his selfishness in putting his own feelings before that of the country (and let me tell you that no group of people understood the idea of sacrifice so much as those of us who were in service), the coronation seemed to be a much-needed shaft of sunlight. With the Coventrys to be away from Croome, there was, in truth, very little additional work for most of the staff to do. But I, at least, was to play a part in the great day: my mistress told me that she would need me to travel with her and His Lordship down to London and to help her get ready for the ceremony.

My first task was to find and see to the gorgeous deep red shoulder-to-floor robe that she – as the wife of one of England's most senior hereditary peers – had to wear. When I located it and went to lift it off its hanger, I let out a gasp of astonishment and nearly fell over: not because of its magnificence – though the velvet fabric was exquisite, the colour like nothing I had ever laid eyes on, and the trim of ermine softer to the touch than I would have thought possible. No, it was the sheer weight of the robe which was truly astounding. How could anyone possibly bear this on their backs for a few minutes, let alone the many hours I knew my mistress would have to wear it? Once again I was struck by just how strong Milady was.

Of course, the garment hadn't been used for many decades – I think, in fact, it was something handed down from one Countess to the next – and needed a few nips, tucks and tweaks here and there. I can tell you that, as I laid the fabulous robe on my bed, never have I taken more care and never was my needlework so neat and precise. It felt like an enormous honour simply to touch this magnificent velvet and the prospect of my young fingers doing some careless damage filled me with dread. But happily, my hand steadied and my needle stayed true and, when I brought it back to my mistress, she expressed herself pleased with my labours.

'Now, Mulley, we shall travel to London the day before

the Coronation. We shall be staying at the house of my sister, Lady Suffield. His Lordship's mother is sending her man to drive us: London is a long way and Roland has never been there and so will not know the streets.'

Well, I was a bit disappointed in that. It would have been lovely for Roland to have driven us down – not just for me but because he would have seen the sights of half of London decked in ribbons and bunting. I was sad he would miss this but then Milady surprised me again.

'The BBC is, it seems, planning to film the Coronation and to show it on the new television service. I am hopeful that all the staff who remain here at Croome will be able to find someone with a set and to watch the Coronation on it. His Lordship has given the servants the day off to mark the occasion.'

Now, here was a thing! We had all heard about the BBC's new television service but it was only available in very limited areas and, of course, no one that any of us knew could afford the enormous price of one of the television sets. I made a mental note to ask Mr Latter if there was some arrangement to be made. And then it dawned on me that, in attending the Countess on the great day, perhaps I might be captured on film and people across the country might see me. I wasn't sure how I felt about that idea but I decided to write to Mum and Dad to let them know.

'When we arrive in London,' my mistress continued, 'I will need you to go to the bank and draw out my jewels. Lady Suffield's chauffeur will accompany you and you must sign a paper to say you have received them. You will take care of them, won't you? They are terribly valuable.'

Needless to say, that got my heart beating faster all over again. I'd never been to the big city and, as far as I was concerned, all I knew about London came from newsreels and gangster movies. Yet here I was being trusted to withdraw goodness-knows-how valuable items. What if I got robbed? Or dropped something? It was one thing cleaning and polishing Milady's jewels here at Croome but at least they never left the four solid walls of her boudoir while I was responsible for them. It was quite a different matter to carry a King's ransom across London – and on the day of the Coronation itself to boot. 'Hilda, my girl, this is quite a pickle you've got yourself into,' was the thought running through my mind. 'But you're just going to have to get your chin up, put your best foot forward and not let anyone down.'

Just as the Countess had said, on the morning before the Coronation a big Black Bentley – much grander than the Coventry's Standard 20 – swept up the driveway to the front of the Court and the Earl, his wife and I were seated in the back. Somehow the succession of suitcases containing their clothes was stowed away in the boot and, with a purr of its powerful engine, the car set off for London. I was terribly excited but it wouldn't have done to have shown this, so I sat demurely, speaking only when spoken to and generally trying to be as invisible as was possible in the confined space.

The 10th Earl had done away with the expense of maintaining a London address. But Lady Suffield was plainly less pressed financially, for her house turned out to be one of those great Georgian places in one of the nobbiest streets in London. As was usual, the servants' entrance was down a steep flight of steps underneath the main front door. I made my way down them, praying that I wouldn't come a cropper again, while struggling with my suitcase. A footman took the Earl and Countess's luggage: at least I didn't have to lug them inside as well.

I was a bit surprised to find that the room I was allocated was tiny and rather poky – the difference, I supposed, between living in the crowded terraces of London, rather than the space and grandeur that I had become used to. And I didn't find Her Ladyship's servants noticeably friendly. But nothing could spoil the tremendous thrill I felt at what was to happen on the morrow. I had been excused my normal morning duties of bringing tea and running my mistress's bath. Instead, I was instructed to be outside the servants' entrance at 9am sharp, respectably attired in hat, coat and gloves. At the appointed hour I ensured my modest little hat was pinned to my hair and that the seams of my stockings were perfectly straight. On the dot of nine, Lady Suffield's chauffeur appeared at the wheel of the great Bentley. It felt very strange to be sat in the back just like one of the gentry, and there was a little glass window between the driver and me, which rather put paid to any conversation.

Off we went through the streets of the capital. On every pavement and at every corner the entire population of London seemed to have come out and be waiting for a glimpse of someone – anyone – who was part of the procession. I sunk down into my seat, not wanting anyone to think that inside the black Bentley there was a person to stare at and cheer.

I couldn't tell you where the bank was – or even what its name was. The chauffeur escorted me into a big open hall that seemed as hushed and as reverential as a church. I barely spoke – and when I did, it was in a whisper – as I signed the papers to collect the Countess's jewels. And when I saw what was written on the bottom of the document – the value of the items in my care was £20,000 (£2 million at today's prices) – I was so terrified I could barely breathe. I couldn't wait to get back to the sanctuary of the Bentley and I didn't dare move a muscle again until I had handed over the whole lot to my mistress.

As we laid them out, one by one, my eyes must have

opened wider and wider. These were not merely beautiful jewels – the like of which I had never seen – but they looked like something out of a storybook. There was even a slender diamond tiara sparkling in the morning light. I knew I would have a lot to tell Mum ad Dad in that day's letter home. It took nearly two full hours to prepare my mistress and, when we were finished and she joined His Lordship on the steps of Lady Suffield's house, I could have burst with pride. I had never seen anyone look so glamorous, so regal and so refined, and I felt truly privileged to have played my part.

Because the robes were so cumbersome and the risk of them being crushed or creased so great, I was to ride in the Bentley to Westminster Abbey with the Coventrys. Once again I drove through the streets of London and heard the cheers of the crowd, saw the sea of little paper flags being waved and had to pinch myself to make sure I wasn't dreaming. 'This is a long way from Number 5, Vine Street, Stamford, Hilda Mary Mulley,' I thought. 'A very long way indeed and no mistake.'

As the car pulled up at the Abbey, I jumped out, ready to assist Milady and catch the back of her robe as she stepped on to the pavement. And then she and His Lordship walked calmly past the wildly cheering throng and into the cool darkness of the historic building.

'Hop back in sharpish, please, miss,' the chauffeur said.

'We need to scarper from here before we block the place up solid. And if we get a bit of a move on, we can be back in time to watch the procession.' He was as good as his word: I got back to Lady Suffield's residence in time to join a crowd of her servants perching precariously on the edge of the house's top-floor windows and straining to catch a glimpse of the magnificent pageantry as it paraded past our very eyes.

'Not many people get such a bird-eye's view of something so important,' I told myself. 'You'll remember this for the rest of your life.' And I'm pleased to say that I was not wrong.

That evening all of the servants crowded round the wireless set to witness another first: King George VI was making an address to the nation on the BBC.

It is with a very full heart I speak to you tonight. Never before has a newly crowned King been able to talk to all his peoples in their own homes on the day of his coronation. Never has the ceremony itself had so wide a significance.

I was astonished as I sat there listening to the King. Not just because it felt like he was talking directly to me – or at least to the whole country, which included me – but because his speech seemed awfully slow and laboured. His brother's abdication address hadn't sounded like this: maybe that's because he wasn't meant to be King and this, today, is what a real monarch sounds like. I couldn't have known then that King George had a terrible stammer and that just getting the words out past his lifelong speech impediment was a truly heroic battle for a man who was just as shy as me.

I felt that the whole empire was in very truth gathered within the walls of Westminster (pause) Abbey. I rejoice that I can now (pause) speak (pause) to you all (long pause) wherever (pause again) you may be … in this personal way, the Queen and I wish health and happiness to you all, and we do not forget at this time of celebration those who are living under the shadow of sickness (a silence which seemed to last forever) and to them I would send a special message of sympathy (another pause) and good cheer.

Well, at that we did cheer. Partly out of loyalty to our country and our King; partly out of gratitude that he had finally got the words out. And then he continued with two sentences that filled me — filled all of us — with a pride in being British, which, had we but known it, we would need to rely on before too many years had passed. 'To many millions the Crown is a symbol of unity. By the grace of

Chapter Eleven

'My Roll'

1938 began much in the same way as the previous year. The first dark shadow on my life appeared via the unusual event of a telephone call for me at Croome Court. The telephone in the servants' quarters was strictly under the control of Mr Latter. The ungainly, stick-like instrument sat outside his room in the long echoing corridor and all of us – whether head servant or housemaid – knew that only he could grant the privilege of making or receiving a call. Whether because of my station in the hierarchy or whether from his habitual kindness, knowing that unlike the rest of the staff I was a long way from home, Mr Latter did let me use the telephone to speak with Mum and Dad. Of course, they didn't possess one themselves but an arrangement had been reached whereby I would place a call to Aunt Beat at the Crown Hotel and she would nip out to bring my parents to the receiver.

But an unscheduled phone call for me was distinctly rare and, from the moment Mr Latter came to find me, I knew that it couldn't be good news. Growing up in Stamford my best friend had been a girl called Mary Russell: we had gone to school together and played together and we were inseparable right up until the time I left to go into service. While I was away we would write to each other and she told me that she had a boyfriend who had asked for her hand in marriage. I was thrilled – she was the first person I knew and loved to be engaged.

It was my Dad on the phone. 'Molly,' he said (like all my family, he still called me by my childhood nickname), 'do you think Her Ladyship would give you leave to come home for a few days? There's been an accident.'

Even as I think about this now, my eyes fill with tears and my mind wonders at the appalling stroke of ill luck – quite literally as it turned out – which befell my closest friend. It's the sort of random accident that today might make headlines in your local paper or an item on the local news: Mary Russell had been electrocuted in the bath.

It seemed that she had been having a bath when a terrible and violent electrical storm landed right on top of Stamford. Amid ear-piercing peals of thunder, a bolt of lightning had hit her house and had somehow ended up earthing itself on her bath water. She had been killed instantly.

I can't remember what I said to Dad, or even if I was capable of saying anything. Big sobbing tears seemed to belch out from my slight frame and I shook with the pain of them. Mr Latter must have wondered what this terrible news was and I think he took the phone from me, told Dad that he was see to it I placed a call back shortly and sat me down in his room. Winnie probably brought me a cup of tea — a big steaming cup of tea, stirred stiff with sugars was the ground state of first aid in those days — though I don't remember drinking it. And the more I thought about poor Mary, the more I sobbed and the more Mr Latter grew alarmed.

He must have slipped away and found the Countess at some point because a little while later he returned to tell me that I was to have a few days off immediately and that I must make arrangements to go home to Stamford so that I could be at the funeral and (just as importantly) so Mum and Dad could take care of me.

'But what about Her Ladyship?' I asked. 'What will she do and who will take care of her?'

'Do not concern yourself with that, Miss Mulley,' Mr Latter told me kindly and calmly. 'All will be taken care of, and the most important thing is to get you home directly.'

Well, I was taken aback: I'd never heard of any of the

servants at Croome being given time off. We weren't even given our birthdays off and, although we would have been allowed to attend a family funeral, Mary wasn't a relative, let alone a close one and, no matter how cut up I was, in the normal scheme of things I would have been expected to take it on the chin and carry on. As things turned out, I wasn't actually given time off: my mistress had merely agreed for me to take a few days of my one week's holiday a little early. Still, at least she let me go.

I was shaken by Mary's death: it was my first encounter with the passing of someone I knew and cared about and it hit me hard. Even when I returned to the Court I couldn't shake the feeling that we were somehow all living under a curse – or at least were going through a spell of truly rotten luck.

The misfortune carried on. My romance with Roland – or Roll as he was to me now that I knew him much better – had continued, although we had to be very careful about keeping it under the strictest of wraps, at least from the Countess. Mr Latter, of course, spotted the signs and was very good about keeping mum, but he did let me know that, if Her Ladyship found out, it would not go well for me.

'You know the rules, Miss Mulley. Fraternisation between the servants is not permitted at Croome. And whilst you are young and I have no wish to be, as you might say, a wet blanket, you must know that, if the veil of discretion ever slips and word reaches the Countess, I should not, I fear, be able to help you.'

But I was young and Roland and I were falling in love. I think our romance had really started during those times he drove me to Worcester for my hairdressing course and, the more we had got to know one another, the more it seemed silly to deny our feelings. We began not just to look forward to our Sunday lunches at his parents' home but to feel they were an essential part of our lives.

I suppose it was inevitable – even without the run of bad luck that seemed to have dogged the lives of everyone at the Court – that we would be found out sooner or later. But I don't think either of us could have imagined the dramatic way our secret would be exposed.

Our Sunday jaunts to Severn Stoke always followed the same routine. After church Roland would fetch his big leather coat and his motorcycle and wait for me a little way off from the house. We had grown used to meeting secretly in the Temple and the Rotunda (my early hopes for their romantic potential had been realised!) and it was easy to find a place to rendezvous in the vast Croome estate. At the start of the year Roland had bought a leather coat for me to wear while clutching on to him on the pillion. And, as it happened, it was a good job he did – though I wish we'd had helmets as well.

One Sunday just like any other we met up, set off and

were puttering along happily with nothing more on our minds than the prospect of a big nourishing lunch and an afternoon of walking hand in hand through the fields. The road that leads into Severn Stoke had – and has to this day – a very sharp hairpin bend, just beside the pub. As we turned the corner, rumbling along at a decent lick, we saw a beer lorry parked sideways across the entire width of the road. There was no chance of braking and no chance of going round it: without a shadow of doubt we were heading straight for its middle.

Somehow – I don't know to this day how he did it – Roland managed to slide the bike over and we slipped sidewise underneath the lorry and shot out the other side. But we didn't emerge unscathed: as the motorbike hit the ground, we were dragged along on our backs and sides, the rough road surface tearing into us with a vengeance. When we came to rest in a ditch on the other side our leather coats were in taters – and Roland had broken several bones.

People poured out of the surrounding cottages and rushed to our aid. The good news was that we were alive: the less good news was that many of those who were patching up our wounds worked at the Court. There was, we realised glumly, no chance of keeping our romance secret any longer.

Roland was more seriously injured than I and had to be excused his duties until he mended. As for me, it was time to face the music. The next morning I took Milady her morning cup of tea, knowing that she couldn't fail to notice the very visible evidence of my accident.

'Gracious, Mulley, what have you been up to? You look like you've been in the wars!'

I started to stammer out an explanation, involving Roland's parents, the Sunday lunch and the ill-fated motorbike journey. 'Here it comes,' I thought. 'You'll be on the next train to Stamford, Hilda Mulley, and serve you right.' But it didn't turn out like that at all. There was – I swear it – a twinkle in my mistress's eye.

'Ah, yes – the dashing chauffeur. Someone rather close to your heart, I think, Mulley. Well, do tell him to be a little more careful with you next time, please. I should not like to lose you now that you are so good at your duties.'

I couldn't believe my ears: the Countess had known all along that I was being romanced by the family chauffeur! And what's more, she didn't seem to mind – or, at least, didn't mind as long as it didn't stop me attending to her. I wasn't going to get the sack after all. Neither, by the sound of it, was Roland. I couldn't wait to tell him what a lucky escape we'd had all round!

When I look back at this – and at other aspects of life at Croome – I realise that, in many ways, the Earl and the Countess were very modern in their thinking. This was to be seen in little things – the fact that Roland didn't have to wear a traditional chauffeur's uniform or the care with which they ensured that we were kept warm in the depths of winter at the Court – as well as the much more surprising moments, such as Milady's acceptance of the love affair between two of her servants. When I compare this to the accounts of life at other great houses – which I would hear from visiting staff or when we, in turn, went to stay in the mansion's of other gentry – I realise how fortunate we were. The 10th Earl had plainly decided to take up where his grandfather had left off and to win the affection of those who served the family by mixing firmness with kindness.

But then, too, I wonder if there wasn't also a bit of the cold blasts of a wind from the world outside that had crept into Croome Court and which the master and my mistress had heeded. For, as 1938 wore on, the clouds began to darken over England and perhaps the aristocracy knew that their time was coming to an end.

As the months of 1938 wore on, the news coming from Europe grew ever more disturbing. We read it every day in the newspapers: His Lordship took *The Times* and every morning Mr Latter would iron this carefully so as to ensure that the Earl had a pristine paper, with no folds or creases, to open after his breakfast. By the end of the day this, along with any other newspapers which the household might have ordered, had made its way down to the servants' quarters. And each day the news seemed worse and the clouds of war that had hung in the air for so long grew darker.

the King himself. Mosley was young, good looking and as haughty and imperious as any aristocrat could be. His father was a cousin (once removed) of the new Queen and he had been in and out of governments of various political hues by the time he formed the British Union of Fascists in 1932.

Mosley's followers were – to my mind and that of many of my fellow servants – a pretty bad lot: they were a motley crew of the worst type of aristocrat and groups of violent thugs, who wore a black uniform and had a nasty habit of beating up anyone who didn't conform to their idea of what Englishmen should be. If you've seen the series of *Upstairs Downstairs* set in the 1930s, you will have seen that the chauffeur was an active blackshirt. Well, I can tell you that nothing would have persuaded our chauffeur – or 'my Roland' as I now thought of him – to be part of anything so obviously nasty as Mosley's fascists. And if truth be told, I don't think the Earl would have allowed it: politics wasn't exactly forbidden at Croome and, provided our opinions and loyalties – whatever they might be – stayed below stairs and didn't disturb the smooth running of the Coventrys' lives, we were pretty much free to think what we liked. But I'm as sure as I can be that, had one of the male servants started marching about in a silly black uniform on his days off, Mr Latter would have come down on him like a ton of bricks.

Mosley himself stomped up and down the country holding melodramatic mass meetings in a pale imitation of his hero, Adolf Hitler. He turned up in Worcester several times in the years that I was at Croome, holding big – and well-attended – events, in which he shouted and postured and his bully boys in black kept order in the most brutal of ways. Not a single one of the staff at Croome went to hear him, I'm proud to say. And whilst it would have been common in earlier years for a baronet like Mosley to stay at the house of one of his fellow aristocrats, he never crossed the threshold at Croome. I'm not sure that we would have been able to hold our tongues if he had!

In any event, the Earl and the Countess seemed to be doing much less in the way of entertaining that year. In part, I think this was down to a general and increasing shortage of money and, in part, because, as the fears of a coming war increased, the gentry seemed to retreat into itself a little and visits to one another's houses grew less frequent. But there was another reason too and it was the answer to the mystery of why the Earl so often missed riding to hounds or left the Countess to go out to dinner with his brother as chaperone. His Lordship, it appeared, had a little bit of a problem with drink.

Now, of course, nothing was ever said officially about this: it would have been literally unthinkable for it to be spoken of openly above stairs. Even in those moments when my mistress seemed closest to me and, as I brushed and rebrushed all that long lustrous hair, shared a few small intimacies, she never once came close to confiding in me about the master's health. Instead, and as I look back and remember our conversations, she would refer to it obliquely.

'His Lordship is unwell again today, Mulley.' Or, 'His Lordship is suffering a little with his nerves and so I shall be riding alone in the morning.'

But in the servants' hall, when Mr Latter's back was turned or he wasn't around to hear, there would be whispers about the Earl's drinking and the effect this was having on his health. I had occasion to see for myself what those effects were when, one morning, Milady told me we were to go away for a few days.

'We are to motor down to Wales tomorrow, Mulley. We shall be staying with friends and I want you to pack clothes suitable for hunting as well as my usual wardrobe.'

It seemed a long way to go just to chase a few different foxes across the countryside: after all, the Countess seemed to have little trouble in finding quarry here at home and did so several days every week in the season. Still, it wasn't my place to question and so I assured her that black jacket, jodhpurs and stock would be packed and ready.

'Oh, Mulley, I shan't be riding to hounds.' She said this as if the idea was the most foolish thing she'd ever heard. 'Otter hunting, Mulley: otters. That is what we shall be doing.'

I'd never heard of hunting otters (although my mistress seemed to think I should have done). But in the 1930s it was a great favourite of the landed gentry and Britain supported 12 full hunts, each as important in their field as the Croome Hunt was in its. You'll know by now that I wasn't a great one for any sort of hunting and kept as far away from the whole business as possible. I certainly didn't intend being any part of what my mistress had planned in Wales. While writing this book I've had to look up just what an otter hunt involved. And I have to say that it hasn't changed my opinion one little bit.

The sport (if that's what you could call it) goes back to the days of King Henry II. He appointed a King's Otterhunter in 1170 and all the monarchs who came after him kept up royal packs of otterhounds until 1689. This possibly explains why there was so much pomp and sporting ceremony involved in the business: each hunt wore different 'colours' and the gentry who belonged to them would travel hundreds of miles to be involved.

The day began at first light when the hunters, carrying long poles to feel their way across rivers and ditches, set off in search of their quarry. They would be accompanied by packs of specially bred hounds, trained to follow the otter even in the long periods when it submerged from sight and tried to get away under water. These hounds were taught to follow the scent of the otter as it rose to the surface of the water and then 'swim' him for as long as six hours until they forced the exhausted creature to land. At this point the hounds would move in for the kill and the master of the hunt would sound the death knell on his hunting horn. Then the master would cut trophies off the otter: first the rudder, or tail; then the mask, or head; and finally the four pads, or paws. These were distributed to followers of the hunt.

Now I don't know about you but, to me, that sounds barbaric and, even by the time I was in service to the Countess, there was strong feeling in the country that it should be stopped. Sadly, it wasn't and, by the time someone got round to making the poor otter a protected species in the 1970s, it had been hunted to near extinction.

This, then, was what Milady had planned for the trip to Wales. And, after explaining what breeches and oilskins would be needed, she gave me further unwelcome news: His Lordship was to drive us down.

It was the first time I had been in the car with the Earl at the wheel. Rumour had it below stairs that this was not an experience to be looked forward to – and that's exactly how it turned out. I had never felt so frightened as His Lordship drove – at speed and somewhat erratically – down the narrow country roads with their sharp bends. Perhaps because of the accident I'd had on Roland's motorbike, I imagined death waiting for us around every blind corner and wished we could slow down. You have to remember that roads then were far less well-constructed than they are now and that, whilst a 30mph speed limit had been (rather reluctantly) introduced a few years before, most police forces had made very public promises that they wouldn't be enforcing it. I suppose that, since only the gentry could afford cars, the police were reluctant to stop those whom they regarded as their betters.

So we swerved and speeded all the way to Wales, stopping, I think, for a bite to eat and a drink (no laws against drink-driving, much less breathalysers, back then) somewhere en route. I sat in the back and wished fervently that it was my Roland at the wheel, not His Lordship. By the time we came back – otter hunts would often last as long as nine whole days – I was very glad indeed to see Croome Court. But no sooner was I feeling safe again than the world changed and we inched closer to war.

It is hard to explain to a generation – or rather at least two generations – which has grown up largely free of the fear of war just how terribly each and every one of us felt the crisis, each and every day. I was born during the last world war and my little brother was now approaching an age where he might be called up to fight. For the rest of the servants, all had lost relatives in the mechanised carnage of the Great War – losses that left deep and indelible mental scars. So we followed each new development with mounting alarm.

The crisis had begun a few months earlier when Hitler began provoking trouble in another country on Germany's borders – Czechoslovakia. Now, I doubt that any of us in the servants' quarters could have told you where that was – don't forget our schooling had been pretty basic and geography tended to concentrate on the great expanse of the British Empire – but I think we all knew something dangerous was afoot. The British government certainly did and, as the crisis worsened, on 22 September the Prime Minister, Neville Chamberlain, took the then unusual step of flying out for a conference with Hitler: his sole aim, he said, was to find a way to stop another war. I really don't think it is an exaggeration to say that almost every British citizen held his or her breath for the next eight days. Finally, Chamberlain flew back, arriving at Heston Aerodrome (this was long before the days when London had a proper airport). As his little plane landed, the waiting press pushed forward to discover whether we were to have peace – or war. Standing beside the tailplane, Chamberlain held aloft a little piece of paper.

The settlement of the Czechoslovakian problem, which has now been achieved is, in my view, only the prelude to a larger settlement in which all Europe may find peace. This morning I had another talk with the German Chancellor, Herr Hitler, and here is the paper, which bears his name upon it as well as mine.

Some of you, perhaps, have already heard what it

contains but I would just like to read it to you: '…We regard the agreement signed last night and the Anglo-German Naval Agreement as symbolic of the desire of our two peoples never to go to war with one another again.'

Later the same day, the Prime Minister stood outside Number 10 Downing Street and repeated the very welcome reassurance. 'My good friends, for the second time in our history, a British Prime Minister has returned from Germany bringing peace with honour. I believe it is peace for our time. We thank you from the bottom of our hearts. Go home and get a nice quiet sleep.'

I cannot describe how wonderful that news felt. I think there was cheering in the servants' hall – although in the steward's room I think there was a more refined expression of relief. Chamberlain's most famous phrase, repeated on the wireless and in all the newspapers, was 'peace for our time'. And goodness knows we were desperate for that peace.

The very next day, Hitler went back on the promises he had given. German troops marched into the northern part of Czechoslovakia called Sudetenland (another place we had to look up in an atlas). It seemed the little piece of paper on which we had placed such store meant absolutely nothing to the Fuhrer. This was followed by reports the next month of two nights of terror in which Nazi-led mobs smashed, burned and looted Jewish shops and synagogues across Germany and Austria. We were now glued to the wireless each evening to hear the BBC's increasingly grave news bulletins. As Christmas approached, the prospects for the New Year looked, if that were possible, even bleaker than in 1938.

Still, we were determined that, whatever the storms slowly gathering, below stairs at Croome Coourt would see the Christmas in with our traditional party. Now, in all honesty, this was very little different to the servants' ball but the Christmas Party – held on the great day itself – was a time solely for the staff: the Earl and the Countess didn't grace us with their presence and for this we were all rather grateful. Now matter how modern our master and mistress might be, the fact is that having them downstairs felt like a bit of an intrusion. We wouldn't dream of being upstairs in their quarters unless there was work to do, so them coming down to our halls rather emphasised that this was work, not pleasure.

But, as I say, the Christmas party didn't involve the gentry and – despite Mr Latter's teasing of Winnie about her cooking – it was something we all looked forward to. We all of us mixed in and helped out: it wouldn't do to leave all the work to Winnie and even Mr Latter rolled up his sleeves and got stuck in.

The meal itself was the traditional Christmas fare – roast

turkey with the full trimmings. I have to tip my hat to the Earl and the Countess, they did us proud and Winnie and Mr Latter were told to spare no expense on provisions. In previous years we had sometimes been joined for the meal by the servants from Pirton Court – the home of His Lordship's mother a few miles away across the fields. And from what they let slip, our master and mistress were a good deal more generous when it came to Christmas lunch below stairs than they were used to. But both Mr Latter and Winnie had been around long enough to know what the score was: although there were a few more treats than we would have through the rest of the year, they never went over the top or pushed our luck.

There was – of course – no alcohol. That's another thing that always strikes me as completely wrong in the television dramas: they seem to be opening bottles of beer or sneaking a few sips of port at every possible opportunity. I can honestly say that below stairs at Croome Court was always strictly teetotal. Tea – the cup that cheers, as the old advert said – was the only drink we ever saw.

But there would be games – parlour games involving all the staff: pass the parcel or charades were the favourites. And it was during one of these games that Christmas 1938 lived up to the spirit of the year itself. Somehow – I still don't know how – Winnie fell down some steps while balancing a cup of tea in her hand. She was quite badly hurt and it took us a long time to settle her down and make sure no bones were broken. 'Here we go again,' I thought. 'It's been a chapter of accidents and it doesn't look like stopping.'

In fact, the only good thing to come out of that whole day was that I discovered I didn't like smoking. Once we had got Winnie sat down, more or less comfortably, someone brought out a packet of Craven A cigarettes: these were one cut above Woodbines – well, it was Christmas – and had a little band of cork around the end you put in your mouth (in those days filters on cigarettes were unheard of), which made it look a little more posh than your average cigarette. It was also widely believed – and this was probably a legacy of the war in the trenches of France – that 'having a gasper' was just the ticket if you'd had a nasty shock.

'Go on, Miss Mulley,' one of the footmen called. 'It'll do you good – and what with the time of year, you should live a bit!'

So I took my first pull on a cigarette – feeling very glad that Mum and Dad weren't here to see such 'fast' behaviour by their eldest daughter – and I coughed and spluttered so much I thought Mr Latter would have to call for the doctor. Even when I recovered from that, I felt horribly sick for the rest of the day and I resolved never, ever to touch a cigarette again. Which is why, I think, I have lived a while: for 97 years, in fact.

Chapter Twelve

War: 'We Have a Clear Conscience'

Sunday, 1 January 1939
Dear Mum and Dad

Happy New Year! I wish that I could be with you and Joan and Jim, but I'm making the best of things here at Croome. Today I went to church as usual in the morning and then Roland Newman took me back to his parents' house for our traditional Sunday lunch. Do write and tell me what you all got up to at home. I miss Stamford and though the fare was very tasty this lunchtime I would have given anything for a jolly good Stamford pie!

How is the weather with you? It is very blowy here and the wind is positively whistling around the Court. The clouds look very threatening and I shouldn't be surprised if we have snow before too many days have passed. I am sitting in front of the coal fire in my bedroom to write to you. At least I'm kept warm!

Do write back when you can and send all my love to Joan and Jim.

Your loving daughter
Molly

The first month of January 1939 was indeed a blustery affair. It was as if the weather was taking its cue from the worsening international situation and was doing its level best to depress the whole country. After an unseasonal burst of mildness, by the end of the month the hills were blanketed in drifts of snow, some of them almost three feet deep. It put a dampener on all our spirits below stairs at Croome Court and for a time stopped even the Countess – normally the hardiest of souls – from venturing out in search of foxes.

When the weather did improve, Milady was back riding to hounds and on occasion she took her oldest children with her. I had seen little of Lady Anne and Lady Joan in my time at Croome because they were generally away at boarding school. I had got to know the two youngest children, Lady Maria and little Bill (as we always called him), and I think we had begun to build quite a real friendship. Although they were mainly the responsibility of Mrs Lovett, the governess, when she had her day off, the little ones came to me. In 1939 Lady Maria was eight years old and a lovely, friendly little thing; Bill was five and a little less loving, but all the same they both liked to come and spend time with me in my big room on the top floor – sometimes when they should have been in the nursery or the schoolroom. I rather think that Mrs Lovett didn't always live up to her name and that the youngsters found me warmer and happier to be with.

The older two girls were by now what we would call teenagers (there was no such word). Lady Anne was 17 and Lady Joan 15, and everything that is difficult and wilful about girls of that age today was concentrated in the younger one – indeed, it was magnified by her privilege and status. I quickly came to realise that my earliest fears about Lady Joan were coming to fruition – and in spades: she was, frankly, a bit of a madam.

This manifested itself mainly in a cast-iron belief that she was allowed to do exactly as she fancied and that no one – certainly not below-stairs staff – could gainsay her. Even a head servant like me or Mr Latter was subject to her whims and her temper.

'Mulley,' she said to me one day – all imperious and haughty – 'Mulley, I want to do this today and you are not to tell me otherwise.' I can't recall exactly what it was but

I knew right enough that it was something she was not supposed to be up to and, if I allowed her to get away with it, my head would be on the block.

'I'm sorry, Lady Joan,' said I. 'You know that Her Ladyship would not permit that, so I am afraid I must say no to you.' I said it as politely as I could (although I didn't feel terribly much like being deferential to this rude little slip of a girl). Still, she was an aristocrat, the daughter of my employer, and a certain courtesy was required of me.

'If you try and stop me, I shall tell Mama and then you will be in trouble,' the little minx pouted. 'In fact, if you dare to get in my way, I shall have you sacked – so there!' Well, my hands were itching: here was a spoiled little madam who needed a fairly swift spanking for her rudeness – and that's exactly what she would have got had she tried anything of that sort with my Mum and Dad. Say what you like about corporal punishment but, when I was growing up, a child jolly well knew his or her place – and cheeking an adult, let alone threatening to have her dismissed from her position, would have been dealt with swiftly and finally with the back of a hairbrush. And I tell you what, people like us learned that lesson from an early age and it served us well in later life.

I must confess that it did cross my kind to give into her little Ladyship: after all, the Countess could be abrupt enough when it came to dealing with her servants and I had no way of knowing if crossing her darling daughter wasn't going to finish up with me out on the big cold step, suitcase in hand and heading back to Stamford in disgrace.

But we Mulleys are made of sterner stuff than that. 'Don't you think about that for one minute, Hilda Mary Mulley,' I told myself sharply. 'Madam here is not going to stamp her pretty little foot and have you dancing to her tune. Even if it isn't a big thing that she wants to do today, give in this one time and she'll have you forever more. Stand your ground – and hope for the best.'

'Well, Lady Joan,' I said, trying to sound more confident than I really felt. 'If that's what you must do, I suggest you go straight to Her Ladyship and do it right away. That way we'll both know who was right, won't we?'

For a moment it looked like she might call my bluff, just as I was trying to call hers. It felt absurd – here was I, a grown woman with a good training in tailoring as well as in life, going toe to toe with a remarkably confident – no, arrogant – young lady of the gentry. I held my breath.

In the finish, she turned on her heel and stalked off in a good old-fashioned paddy. I didn't see her for the rest of the day – 'Sulking,' I thought to myself 'Sulking little a spoiled child.' – and I never heard a word about it from my mistress. I took it, therefore, that I had won and that Lady Joan had thought better of running off to tell tales, let alone get me the sack.

But back in my room that night I did begin to worry. Oh, I was sure I'd been right to stand up to the little madam but there was something in her blazing eyes and unnatural self-importance that boded ill for the future. 'You'll come to a bad end, my proud little Lady,' I thought. 'A very bad end indeed, if you're not careful.'

As spring turned to summer, we all of us had much greater worries on our minds. The clouds of war were gathering and casting a sombre, fearful mood over the whole country. 'If Hitler has his way, we'll be back in the trenches by Christmas,' was the gloomy view of the footmen in the servants' hall – an ironic echo of the optimistic phrase uttered by ordinary people as we prepared for the Great War: it'll all be over by Christmas.

Nowadays I don't think so many people know as much as we did about what was going on the world – even with all the television channels and the Internet and suchlike. I wonder sometimes if anyone knows much about the United Nations and who's doing what in it where, or even if they know what it's for. Well, the United Nations didn't exist yet – it would take another world war to bring it about – but after all the suffering and death of the Great War a League of Nations had been set up to try and ensure world peace. It was a pretty inefficient body, that's for sure, yet people pinned their hopes on it and so we followed the news about its latest failures (and they were legion) with a sort of groaning, inward dread. So when Nazi Germany withdrew from the League, we knew that war was only a matter of time.

Within weeks of Hitler walking out of the League of Nations – 'taking his bat home' was how it was seen below stairs – we had a pretty good idea what would be the spark to set all of Europe aflame again. The strutting little man with the stupid moustache told the world that Germany would no longer honour its promise not to attack Poland. Again, I'm struck by how closely ordinary people followed the news and understood its significance back then. Maybe it's because we didn't have all the sideshow nonsense of celebrity and glamour but everyone knew that Poland was going to be the sticking point. Czechoslovakia had been bad enough but the Prime Minister had managed to buy time, claiming that it was 'a little country far away of which we know nothing'. Well, that was largely true – just as it was of Poland – but it didn't stop us caring and worrying and knowing that, if Britain didn't do something, Hitler was just going to march all over everywhere. Would people of my age today have had the same sort of understanding and reaction? I wonder: I really do.

Not that we had much chance of not knowing something was coming our way. In April the government reinstated conscription for men ages 20 to 21. Not since the end of the Great War 21 years earlier had Britain set in train a mass mobilisation of the nation's young men: it was the first peacetime conscription in British history. The first stage was a requirement for them to register for six months of military training but we all knew that this was only a preliminary to the real business of building up a full-time army strong enough to take on Hitler and the Nazis.

Mum wrote to me in the summer to let me know that call-up papers had arrived for Jim. It felt terrible. Jim was my little brother and the person I'd been closest to growing up. How could he be going away to train as a soldier? But he was and I felt useless and powerless to give him any sort of comfort, stuck miles out in the country at Croome as I was.

As if to spite us, the weather turned very warm and blessed the country with a beautiful summer. As Roland and I walked out around the Croome estate, sitting peacefully by the river, lulled by its gentle noises and warmed by the sun on our backs, I looked around and thought, 'What will happen to all this? Surely it won't all be swept away?' But I think I knew in my heart of hearts that the coming war would change England – the old, slow, traditional England with its quaint ways and its rigid class system – and change it forever.

The news on the wireless was our constant companion.

I don't think there was a single bulletin that wasn't listened to in total silence. But just as the plummy tones of the announcer delivered bad news after bad news, the BBC came up with something inspired to keep our spirits up. It was called ITMA – and I think it was one of the most important weapons we had on the home front for the entire war. ITMA stood for 'It's That Man Again'. This had originally been a wonderfully sarcastic headline about Hitler in the *Daily Express* as he strutted about Europe, shouting and posturing. I like to think that this determination to poke fun at the man who was turning all of Europe into a bloodbath was typical of the English spirit of pluck – 'It's that man again. Doesn't he look ridiculous?' Anyway, the BBC took the headline and turned it into the title of a radio comedy series, starring Tommy Handley, then the nation's favourite funny man.

The programme was written as close as possible to transmission because the BBC wanted the scripts to lighten the effect of the latest news with a little gentle send-up. It featured dozens of characters with silly names – Mrs Mopp, the cleaner and Colonel Chinstrap, who was just what you imagine him to be. I read later that the pompous old soldier on whom the character was based was an avid listener to the programme but totally failed to connect the character with himself, and commented, 'Wonderful character. I knew silly buggers like that in India.'

These characters became a vital part of what we would today call the national consciousness. I don't think there was a person in the land who didn't know about Mona Lott, the depressed laundrywoman, or Ali Oop, the Middle Eastern salesman. And the show's catchphrases were adopted by the whole country – rich and poor. Everywhere you went you heard, 'It's being so cheerful as keeps me going,' 'I don't mind if I do,' and, 'TTFN – Ta Ta For Now.' One of the most famous – 'After you, Claude. No, after you, Cecil.' – was a natural for below-stairs staff, but would also be taken up by RAF pilots as they queued for attack on German planes during the Battle of Britain.

ITMA, then, was an antidote to all the dire news piling up on everyone's doorstep. And as August slid to a balmy end, we were going to need as much of that antidote as we could swallow, in the face of Germany's naked intention to invade Poland – we had all been shocked to read that August how Hitler had called a meeting of his military leadership at Obersalzberg and, in a chilling speech, given instructions to 'kill without pity or mercy all men, women, and children of the Polish race or language'. If any of us had harboured any doubts, this was the moment we knew we were up against a madman. At the end of the month our country and France signed an agreement to come to Poland's aid in the event of an attack. When we heard the news on the wireless in the servants' hall, we all looked at one another: this was the last chance for peace. Faced with fighting another war with Britain, would Hitler back down or return the world to carnage?

On the morning of Sunday, 3 September 1939, the BBC advised the nation to wait by its sets to hear a broadcast by the Prime Minister, Neville Chamberlain. We would normally have all trooped up to Croome church for the compulsory service – and done so willingly, since prayers to the Almighty seemed our best hope in this dark time. Instead, we clustered around the wireless. At 11.15am the Prime Minister spoke to the people, rich and poor, commoner and aristocrat, servant and master.

This morning the British Ambassador in Berlin handed the German Government a final note stating that, unless we heard from them by 11 o'clock that they were prepared at once to withdraw their troops from Poland, a state of war would exist between us. I have to tell you now that no such undertaking has been received, and that consequently this country is at war with Germany.

You can imagine what a bitter blow it is to me that all my long struggle to win peace has failed. Yet I cannot believe that there is anything more or anything different that I could have done and that would have been more successful.

Up to the very last it would have been quite possible to have arranged a peaceful and honourable settlement between Germany and Poland, but Hitler would not have it. He had evidently made up his mind to attack Poland whatever happened, and although he now says he put forward reasonable proposals, which were rejected by the Poles, that is not a true statement. The proposals were never shown to the Poles, nor to us, and, although they were announced in a German broadcast on Thursday night, Hitler did not wait to hear comments on them, but ordered his troops to cross the Polish frontier.

His action shows convincingly that there is no chance of expecting that this man will ever give up his practice of using force to gain his will. He can only be stopped by force.

We and France are today, in fulfilment of our obligations, going to the aid of Poland, who is so bravely resisting this wicked and unprovoked attack on her people. We have a clear conscience. We have done all that any country could do to establish peace. The situation in which no word given by Germany's ruler could be trusted and no people or country could feel themselves safe has become intolerable. And now that we have resolved to finish it, I know that you will all play your part with calmness and courage.

At such a moment as this the assurances of support that we have received from the Empire are a source of profound encouragement to us. The Government have made plans under which it will be possible to carry on the work of the nation in the days of stress and strain that may be ahead. But these plans need your help. You may be taking your part in the fighting services or as a volunteer in one of the branches of Civil Defence. If so you will report for duty in accordance with the instructions you have received. You may be engaged in work essential to the prosecution of war for the maintenance of the life of the people – in factories, in transport, in public utility concerns, or in the supply of other necessaries of life. If so, it is of vital importance that you should carry on with your jobs.

Now may God bless you all. May He defend the right. It is the evil things that we shall be fighting against – brute force, bad faith, injustice, oppression and persecution – and against them I am certain that the right will prevail.

I looked around the servants' hall. Mr Latter, Winnie Sapstead, Mrs Lovett: all the head servants; the footmen, the housemaids – I saw a tear glistening Dorothy Clarke's eye – the kitchen and scullery maid, and my own dear Roland. No one said a word. Each was looking inward, thinking of family and loved ones, as I was of Jim, my little brother who would now, I knew, be called upon to fight and to kill and to face men – boys – just like him who would be trying to fight and kill him.

We were at war. And nothing would ever be the same again.

Chapter Thirteen

To the ATS and Farewell to Croome

Daily Express, Saturday, 8 May 1948
LADY JOAN KEPT TITLE SECRET
College riddle of 48 hours off
Express Staff Reporter: Newbury (Berks) Friday

Lady Joan Blanche Coventry, 23-year-old sister of the Earl of Coventry, lived for a month as Miss Coventry, a business student, at Newbury, where she was found dying in an hotel last night.

She left Croome Court, the family seat near Worcester, to register at a commercial college in Netwon Road, Newbury. She wanted to be a business secretary. She told nobody that her father was the 10th Earl of Coventry, killed in action in 1940, or that her 14-year-old brother is the present Earl.

Then on Tuesday she asked the college principal for 48 hours leave. She gave no reason. It was granted and she was due to return to her studies today. Late last night a police surgeon was called urgently to the Chequers Hotel. 'Miss Coventry' was unconscious in bed in her nightdress. At her side was an empty aspirin bottle. An ambulance took her to hospital. She died; and then her identity was discovered.

Said Mrs Spackman, principal of the commercial college: 'Joan was a good mixer, pleasant, and keen to get on. It was a surprise to all of us to learn who she was. We knew her as plain Joan.'

Results of a post-mortem will not be known until tomorrow. A pathologist is making further investigations. Late tonight police were trying to discover why Lady Joan wanted 48 hours off. They were tracing her movements since Tuesday.

Her mother, the Countess of Coventry, today drove from Croome Court to help the police, who were puzzled by another query: why did Lady Joan choose Newbury?

Lady Joan's father was master of the Croome Hunt and she was a fine horsewoman. She often exercised horses at Mr Fred Rimmel's Kinnersley racing stables near Croome. After leaving Malvern school she went into the ATS, in which her mother was Chief

Commandant. Later she was commissioned. Said a friend: 'She was shy and reserved outside her circle. But to us she was charming.'

Nine years had passed since Mr Chamberlain's sombre announcement of a new war with Germany. Nine years – not such a long time in the scheme of people's lives – and no more than a fraction of the time I have been on this planet. But these were nine years in which everything changed: the whole world was in upheaval, lives were uprooted and – all too often – ended, and the social hierarchies of England, which had seemed so certain to continue when a few short years earlier the country had celebrated the coronation of its new King, were shattered and cast to the four winds.

And what of Hilda Mary Mulley, trained dressmaker-tailor turned lady's maid to the mistress of one of the greatest aristocratic houses in the land? My life, too, would be turned upside down and then inside out. The change began a few mornings after the announcement of war. I was taking my mistress her morning cup of tea, preparing her bath and laying out her clothes when the axe fell.

'War has come, Mulley,' Her Ladyship said wistfully. 'It will be a terrible business – perhaps worse than the Great War. It will affect every one of us here at home as well as those poor boys who are sent overseas to fight.' I wondered if she was talking about my brother: Jim was of fighting age to be sure. But then it dawned on me that she had concerns rather closer to home: her husband. The Earl of Coventry was not yet 40 and was sure to volunteer: *noblesse oblige* – the price you paid (for there is always a price for everything) for the privilege of being one of the gentry.

'Everyone must do their bit, Mulley,' my mistress continued and I nodded. 'His poor Lordship,' I thought. He was never the strongest amongst us – why, even the prospect of riding out to hounds with his wife and children would regularly send him scuttling back to his bed and pleading sickness. How would he possibly cope with the hell of warfare? But my concerns were misplaced, for the Countess had other sacrifices in mind.

'I shall, of course, join the ATS. I would like you to volunteer also, Mulley. If we join together, you can be assigned as my batman and I shall not have to do without your services.'

So that was what Her Ladyship meant by sacrifice! She wanted me to join up and she wanted this, or so it seemed, not because I would in some way be serving the country in its darkest hour, but so that I could continue to wait on her hand and foot! Well, I'd heard some things – some cheek in my time – but this took the biscuit. 'You're in a real pickle now, my girl,' I thought as the Countess slipped off to enjoy her hot bath. 'What on earth are you going to do about this little fix?'

So what was this outfit the Countess wanted us to join? The Auxiliary Territorial Service had been set up a year earlier as the government finally saw that war was coming. There had been a similar organisation set up during the Great War – the Women's Auxiliary Army Corps (WAAC) but that had been disbanded in 1921. The ATS was organised much on the same lines as an all-encompassing body for women in uniform. It was attached to the existing men's Territorial Army and, that September of 1939 it, too, was made up of volunteers. That would change in December 1941 when all unmarried women between the ages of 20 and 30 were conscripted into service but, for now, there was – in theory – an element of choice about joining up.

I say an element of choice because the mood in the country was pretty much universally that of everyone wanting 'to do their bit' – that's another phrase I haven't heard for a long, long time: a reminder, perhaps, that in the darkest of hours the nation came together in a way I think we have lost in the decades since. And so there was great – if largely unspoken – pressure from society for girls like me to put King and country before ourselves. But, of course, I was not in the same position as other girls my age. I was a servant to a great lady and, if societal pressure wasn't enough, when the Countess said jump, the only real question was: how high? I sighed inwardly. Without a shadow of a doubt, I was going to have to swap my civilian 'uniform' (if the white pinny I had to wear for the hours spent brushing Milady's hair could be called that) for the khaki dress and skirt of a volunteer woman soldier. Still, I consoled myself with the thought that I would at least still be with my mistress and that my duties were unlikely to be much different – war or no war.

I suppose I should have realised, even then, that my life was about to take a dramatic turn for the worse but I think that, with the terrible fear of war which clouded everyone's mind, I didn't think too deeply about what was to come – and after all, it wasn't as if I had much of a choice. So I wrote home to Mum and Dad with the news that I was going to join up.

When the letter came back from Stamford, it was with the news that my brother Jim had also enlisted. The Military Training Act, which had been introduced in April 1939, had required all men of fighting age to register with the army for a six-month training stint. And when the war broke out, a lot of men – my brother was one of them – volunteered to join up full time. Britain could still only muster an army of 875,000 men and within a month of Chamberlain's speech all men between the ages of 20 and 23 were ordered to report for duty in one of the armed services. You could, in those early days, choose which one you went into – army, navy or air force. Jim plumped for the army and was assigned to the Royal Engineers, the same unit which I think Dad had served in during the First World War. It felt strange and terribly frightening to know that my little brother – and that's how I still thought of him – was now to be a soldier and would before long be setting off to fight Hitler's mighty Nazi military machine. All through the previous two years this had crashed its way into country after country, crushing any opposition in its path: now my Jim was setting off to try and keep it away from the shores of Britain.

Within a day or two of receiving my orders from the Countess, she had been true to her word and joined the ATS. Now it was my turn. I took the bus into Worcester and found the office where I was to sign my papers. I explained to an officious woman in uniform that I was personal maid to the Countess of Coventry, that she had enlisted and that she wanted me to join up too and be assigned as her batman. The woman gave me a look.

'The army will decide where you are posted and who you are attached to, not your present employer – however mighty she might be. Sign here.'

Did I realise even then what I was doing by putting pen to paper and carefully inscribing my signature? You know, I'm not sure that I did.

Within a week or so an official brown envelope arrived at Croome Court addressed to Pvt. H.M. Mulley: my call-up papers. I was ordered to report to Norton Barracks, on the outskirts of Worcester. Did you notice that title the army had assigned me? I was to be a Private – the lowliest rank in all the service. Hardly surprising, I suppose, but there it was nonetheless. I thought that maybe this was the rank assigned to all batmen, whose main job was to look after the officer assigned to them. And that should tell you something else: while I was to enter service as just another member of the rank and file, the Countess was to walk right in as an officer from day one. It was a very peculiar thing – and a sign of the times we lived in back then – that any member of the aristocracy was automatically assumed to be worthy of an officer's rank, while the rest of us were gathered up in the somewhat dismissive catch-all of 'other ranks'.

There was a report in the *Daily Mirror* (the paper of choice for families such as mine, although it would never be seen inside Croome Court!) that rather summed the whole thing up. Under the headline GIRLS IN CAMP, the journalist described a visit to an ATS weekend training camp Her Ladyship had attended.

Militiamen have had a fair amount of limelight recently. So have territorials. No doubt they all deserve it. But what of the girls? Thousands of them, too, have been in camp and their lot has been much harder than that of the young men. They have had to contend not only with cold but with floods. And still there have been no complaints.

A girls' camp has much of that delightful informality and untidy orderliness which one associates with the Portuguese Navy. Whatever may be said against hanging the day's wash from the wireless aerial from an aesthetic point of view, no fault can be found with the idea in practice if the radio still works. And in a girls' camp everything and everybody does work. The Auxiliary Territorial Service at Tidworth Pennings proves that.

Two of the most interesting women there are Countess of Coventry, County Commandant for Worcester, and Lady Elizabet Pleydell-Bouverie, sister of the Earl of Radnor …

Lady Cov, tall, dark, with beautiful brown eyes, was the Hon. Nesta Philipps, Lord and Lady Kylsant's daughter when she married in 1921 aged only 18. Now she is chatelaine of one of England's loveliest homes, Croome Court in Worcestershire.

Two of the visitors to the camp have been Dame Helen Gwnnse-Vaughan, Director of the Service, and the Duchess of Marlborough, who were amazed at the good spirits still prevailing in the washed-out camp.

I don't think anyone would have reported on me as I prepared to do my bit, much less call me 'one of the most interesting' women in any camp. Yet there she was, my mistress and employer, being feted in the press and receiving other equally high-born ladies as 'visitors'. Oh, and for good measure, she had been appointed to the rank of County Commandant.

'Hey ho,' I thought. 'That's just how the world is,' and went to tell my mistress that I had done as she asked and that I had made clear to the ATS that the Countess of Coventry had requested I be assigned to her as a personal servant.

As it turned out, the officious officer at my signing on had been far more astute than either Milady or me. The army, in all its wisdom, had decided that the Countess was to be based at a quite different set of barracks, many miles away from Norton, at Warwick. Her great plan for us to see the war through together – with me still meeting her everyday clothing and bathing needs – was not to bear fruit. For the first time in five years we were to be separated.

Now, maybe that doesn't seem like much to you but you have to remember that I was only 19 when I joined the staff at Croome and my adult life to date had been bound up completely with hers: every part of my day was tied to Milady's needs and wishes. Whilst I could never say that she

replaced my family, in a funny way I was terribly fond of her
– as well as being completely dependant on her too. After all,
my food, my warmth and the very roof over my head were
all part of the job of being in service to a great lady.

That's when it hit me. With my mistress away in one
barracks and me serving at Norton, I was going to have to
leave Croome. There would be no reason for me to stay on
in the lovely big room at the top of the magnificent house
because there would be no Countess living there to serve.
I was going to lose my home and, with it, everything I had
loved. Because I had grown to love the place. I treasured
the times when I was free to wander over the vast estate –
a place of wonder and peace and tranquility. My friends –
such as I had – were other servants: I had barely seen my
old school chums from Stamford in the five years I was in
service. And then there was Roland, the man with whom
I was in love and who had become so precious to me.
What was to happen to our romance? And what would
happen to him?

Roland, of course, volunteered. He was, by then, 35 and,
although men of his age were not yet being called up, he
felt it was his duty. But the army had other ideas about that
too. In those days you had to be assessed by a doctor and
pass a fairly strict medical to enlist. Roland failed, marked
down as medically unfit to serve. It was a terrible blow to
him: men that he knew were already in uniform and being

sent overseas to fight. Even His Lordship, with all his seeming illnesses, was accepted and given a commission.

Poor Roland felt ashamed that he wasn't good enough to serve his country. On top of which he was to lose his job: with the Earl away fighting and the Countess in charge of whatever ATS unit she had been given, there would be no place for a chauffeur at Croome. In fact, there was to be no Croome at all: the great Court was shut up and turned over to the War Department.

The first thing I had to do was to find somewhere to live. With Croome under dust sheets and the idea of living in at Norton Barracks not deemed suitable by the army, I was homeless. Fortunately, Roland's brother Arnold came to the rescue. He offered me digs at the farm where he worked, and one sad day in late September 1939 I took my little cardboard suitcase down from the top of the wardrobe, packed up my few belongings and made ready to say goodbye to life at Croome.

You might think that such a momentous occasion – for that was how it felt to me – would stick in my memory. But the truth is I can't remember a single thing about it. I must have bade farewell to Mr Latter and Winnie and all the under servants; I must have taken one last lingering look at my wonderful bedroom – bigger than I had ever been used to in my life before service; I must, too, have attended one last time to my mistress, brushing her hair and making sure she had everything she would need for the day ahead. Yet I can't recall a single moment of it and, if Her Ladyship said anything to mark our separation or to recognise my years in her service, it has slipped away into the mists of my fading memory. But, you know, I'm not even certain that she did.

Our story must now split into distinct and separate sections – and ones which I have only been able to glue back together in the years since the world descended once again into war. Perhaps they are like the reels of a great film, which have been separated and can at first only be viewed individually.

One reel follows Private Hilda Mulley in her new life at Norton Barracks – and, in truth, that is a short reel. Another shows the war as it tore up the countries of Europe, leaving a generation of young men as names only to be listed in the ever-growing roll call of casualties. While the third will give us a peek into the life of Croome Court when its owners and all their servants have departed. And that, I think, is a very interesting reel indeed. I shall try my best to glue and splice the frames of these films into a single story.

Norton Barracks – a depressing 20-acre hodge-podge of tarmac and Nissen huts (great prefabricated steel buildings) had existed for more than 100 years by the time I reported there for duty. In 1939 the function of the

Depot was to train recruits and administer the 'home' of the Worcestershire Regiment. That training was divided into 'Primary', covering the first six weeks of a new recruit's service, and 'Corps', which concentrated on the more advanced skills they would need to operate as infantry troops in battle. What struck me most of all on my first day in uniform was the sheer number of men gathered there. Everywhere I looked men were marching, or being yelled at by fierce-looking sergeant majors, or running at a sort of half-trot between the various barracks buildings. It seemed like half of the army must be concentrated here and, in fact, their numbers were so great that an old disused jam factory had been requisitioned and a brand-new camp of wooden huts had been constructed at one end of the base. It was to this camp that I was assigned.

You might have thought – and I most certainly did – that my training as a dressmaker-tailor might have been noted and some use found for it. But there's an old saying that the army never actually thinks in straight lines, and so it proved. As I stood before the Commanding Officer that day, I learned that my great service to King and country was going to be waiting on tables in the Officers' canteen – or mess as it was called in the services. It seemed then – and still to this day I feel the same – an act of short sightedness: wasn't there a need for my skills?

I was sure there was and equally sure that my mum and

dad hadn't scrimped and saved to find the £25 for my apprenticeship only to see their daughter wait hand and foot on the dining tables of a bunch of la-di-da officers. Even my five years in service to Her Ladyship had managed to make some use of what I had been trained for. My new role seemed both a great waste of my abilities and an odd way to keep the home fires burning during the country's darkest hours. Still, the army did things its own way and I could have no more budged it from its decision than I could have taken up a gun and had a pop at Hitler myself. I consoled myself that, while I wasn't convinced the army knew best, at least I would be able to make sure the boys who were to go and do the fighting started out with a full stomach and clean tables to eat from.

In that, they were better off – as so they should have been – than the rest of the population. On 8 January 1940 rationing came into force and the people of Britain (me included) began to learn the meaning of tightening your belt. When war broke out, the country was importing an enormous proportion of its food – 20 million tons per year, including more than half of the meat, three quarters of our cheese and sugar, nearly 80% of all fruit and about 70% of cereals and fats. Not surprisingly, Hitler ordered his warships and U-Boats to attack the merchant ships which kept us alive – and barely a day passed without news that a vessel had been sunk.

The first items to be 'on the ration' were bacon, butter and sugar. The government issued every single person in the country a little green ration book, with coupons to tear out and hand over with payment for your allowance. This was followed quickly by meat, tea, jam, biscuits, breakfast cereals, cheese, eggs, lard, milk and canned and dried fruit. Almost all of these controlled items were rationed by weight – an ounce of this or three ounces of that – but meat was rationed by price. We all had to get used to counting our coupons as well as our pennies and eking out the decreasing quantities of the rations became, as the war years ground on, a constant struggle.

The thing everyone hated most was 'the national loaf'. Bread wasn't actually rationed during the war (although it would be after the fighting had ended) but the government ordered bakers to produce a new type of 'national loaf', made of wholemeal flour, which replaced the ordinary white variety we had all been used to. It tasted mushy, looked grey and was widely blamed for causing what might politely be called 'digestion problems': since most of the country didn't have indoor plumbing, you can imagine why this was an issue!

Things got worse when the government issued a new order that bread must not be sold to a customer until the day after it was baked: the idea was to help the country cut down on the amount of bread we ate. Some bright spark in one of the ministries in Whitehall worked out that it was difficult to slice freshly baked bread thinly so our portions were a little too big, and that the tastiness of a loaf fresh from the oven was likely to encourage people to eat too much of it.

Like bread, fish was not on the ration but the price increased considerably as the war progressed and supplies dropped to 30% of pre-war levels. Long queues outside fishmongers became a common sight, and at the good old English fish-and-chip shop. In fact, everywhere you looked there were queues. Housewives – and that was a term you could use in those days without fear of seeming sexist – often spent much of their day lining up in one queue or another in the hope of finding enough to feed their families.

In fairness, it wasn't just the ordinary people like the Mulleys in Stamford and the Newmans in Severn Stoke who were having to live on a much reduced diet. Because rationing was controlled by coupons rather than money, being rich didn't guarantee you a full stomach.

Even for those with enough cash to go to eat out found that the government had seen them coming. In May 1942 an order was passed that meals served in hotels and restaurants must not cost over five shillings per customer and must not be of more than three courses, only one of which could contain meat or fish or poultry.

As the war progressed, other basic commodities joined the ever-growing list of things on the ration. Clothing was rationed on a points system. When it was introduced, on 1 June 1941, no clothing coupons had been issued and, at first, any unused margarine coupons in ration books were valid for clothing. Soon, though, our little ration books had special sections for clothes. Initially, the allowance was enough for one new outfit per year – and that included shoes, hat and gloves – but, as the war progressed, the points were reduced until buying a single item like a coat used almost a year's clothing coupons.

At least in this bit of the war on the home front my training came to the fore. I was able to run up material into something useful and to make new clothes from old ones. And in June 1940 I was to have a very good reason to do so.

But first our attention must turn to the second reel of our film, and to the northern coast of Europe. The Battle of France began in earnest on 10 May 1940. The German Army Blitzkreig had swept through Holland and advanced westward through Belgium. Four days later it burst through the Ardennes forests and advanced rapidly northward to the English Channel. A combination of British, French and Belgian units tried to stop the German spearhead but by 20 May Hitler's troops had reached the coast, splitting each of the three Allied armies off from one another. With their backs, literally, to the sea, the Battle of Dunkirk began: it was a disaster.

The story of how a flotilla of small ships rescued more than 330,000 allied troops has gone down in history as one of the defining moments of Britain during the war. At the time, the full extent of the crisis was kept from us by the official censor, who stopped newspapers publishing details of the unfolding disaster. But the papers – and the wireless – did tell us that the King had called for an unprecedented national week of prayer, and his call was echoed by the Archbishop of Canterbury when he led a special service 'for our soldiers in dire peril in France'.

All of us knew someone – or knew of someone who knew someone – trapped on those beaches at Dunkirk. And we prayed, intensely and gladly, for their safe return. And when, by some miracle – or so it seemed – the gallant little ships succeeded in rescuing our boys from the beaches and getting them under a hail of gunfire and bombs from above to the safety of the navy carriers, we rejoiced and thanked God for his deliverance.

But there was one soldier – one among many, I know, but one whom I had known, whose hand I had shaken and whose bread I had eaten – who did not return. William George, 10th Earl of Coventry died at Dunkirk.

When I heard the news, I confess that I wept and I looked in and amongst my possessions for a little photograph, no more than two inches by two inches in size, which I had taken the summer before. It was a photograph that had got me into a little hot water with Mr Latter but which I treasured as much as anything else I had brought with me from my old life at Croome. It was a picture of His Lordship and my mistress, holding hands with Lady Maria and young Bill, taken at the back of the Court. Milady was wearing a bright, patterned summer dress, her long dark hair tucked up and pinned at the back; the children were smiling shyly and carrying wooden tennis rackets. The Earl himself was staring directly into the camera lens, his trousers hitched high above the waist with braces (as was the fashion in those days) and a smile just visible underneath his wide, sandy moustache.

I remembered Mr Latter's shock and outrage when I asked His Lordship if I might snap their picture. 'Miss Mulley, a servant must never take a photograph of the family – never!' And I recall His Lordship's gentle response that it would be fine this one time for an exception to be made. Now he was gone: a body amongst many bodies, lying somewhere on the bloodied beaches of Dunkirk.

I wondered how my mistress was taking the news. At one time I might have been of some comfort to her in her grief and loss – for, as I have said, I am convinced that she truly loved him. But she was in barracks many miles away and I was stuck waiting on tables at Norton.

As the month of June moved on, however, I had happier thoughts to take the place of grief. For on Saturday, the

15th, I returned to Stamford and to the church of St Michael to be married to Roland Newman. Somehow — goodness knows from where — I had found enough material to make up a white wedding dress with a full-length veil. On my head I wore a tiara — not as priceless as the one I had drawn from the bank for Milady to wear at the coronation but a source of some pride for me nonetheless. In my hands I carried a huge posy of flowers and, beside me, Roland — my Roll — sported a smart carnation in the buttonhole of his three-piece suit.

We didn't, of course, have a honeymoon and our first home was a little terraced cottage in Hatfield, one of the villages near Croome Court: close enough to Norton Barracks for me, and to Worcester itself, where Roland had found work driving a lorry for a local company.

The house itself was a far cry from what we had been used to at the Court. There was no hot running water, no electricity and the days of the luxury of having my morning bath prepared for me by a housemaid were long gone. In those days, for us, posh sanitation meant a non-slippery path to the toilet at the bottom of the back yard! But it was our own home (though rented, never bought) and, if we began our married life amid the privations of war, we were happy just to be with each other.

What of Croome itself in those wartime years? Had we but known it — and it would be a secret kept until long after Hitler had been beaten and peace declared – our old home had been turned into one of the most important places in the whole war.

Shortly after the Coventry family moved out, the RAF moved in and began constructing an aerodrome on the estate. In all, it would take two full years to transform the Croome parkland into RAF Defford and, although it was never an operational flying base, what happened there would be the key to winning the war. In May 1942 scientists and officers moved in – all in conditions of utmost secrecy – and began to establish something called the Telecommunications Flying Unit, or TFU for short. So hurried and so secret was the move to Defford that many of the personnel had, at first, to be accommodated in tents. Before long an entire new set of buildings had been erected to house at least 2,500 personnel, as well as hangers to accommodate 100 aircraft. What was all of this in aid of? One word (although not one we heard, nor would have understood if we had): radar.

Civilian scientists, flying from Defford with aircrews from the Royal Air Force and the Royal Navy, tested the radar systems that were to revolutionise the operational capability of Allied aircraft. From the first early successes with Airborne Interception (AI) systems to Air to Surface Vessel (ASV) radar, which enabled the German U-boat menace to be effectively countered by the end of 1943, the work of the TFU was critical to Britain winning the Battle of the Atlantic and, later, to our bombers being able to target German cities accurately. All in all, without RAF Defford – or Croome Court, as we still thought of it – we might never have won the war, or at least would have paid an even greater price for doing so.

Not, as I say, that Roland and I – or anyone else – knew a thing about it. So secret was the work being carried out at our old home that not a word of it leaked out. Looking back, I find it strange to think of the Croome estate – the place where I met and courted and fell in love with my husband – being so vital in bringing the war to an end.

By the time that end came and I was able to hang up my khaki ATS uniform for the last time, we had been joined in our little cottage by the first of two sons. We christened him Roland Allan, in honour of his father, but the first name never stuck and from his earliest days he was Allan.

It would be nice to say that life changed immediately for the better that day in May 1945 when all of Britain celebrated victory in Europe. But there were still terrible scars left by the war. My brother Jim was one of those who never came home, killed in a tank on the borders of Holland in 1944. A little cross in a military cemetery with his service number – 7635107 – and his rank (Sergeant) is all that marks the contribution he made and the place where he gave his life for King and country. And the privations of wartime life continued long after peace broke out, with rationing reduced but then stepped up as the chill economic winds of the new post-war world blew through the broken and blasted landscape of Britain.

You might wonder, as I did, whether I might have returned to Croome: it certainly crossed my mind in the months after the war's end whether I might receive a summons from Her Ladyship. And, in a manner of speaking, I did.

I had not heard from her at all during the nearly six years we both were in uniform but at some point in 1947 word was sent asking me if I could go up to Croome and visit the Countess. Perhaps you might think that she was about to request that I resume my duties as her maid? Or, failing that, at least to enquire as to my welfare. But no: I was sent for to see if I would undertake a little sewing – a few buttons here, a few repairs there, nothing more than that. Of course, I agreed and in time the little trickle of seamstress work from Her Ladyship was supplemented by the occasional request from Lady Joan. This, too, I was pleased to help with.

As with the Countess, I had not seen Lady Joan since leaving Croome back in 1939. I would like to be able to say that I noticed a change in her – perhaps the war might have made her a little less wilful than before: after all, she had joined up and served with her mother in the ATS. But if I did, I cannot say I recall it. And so, perhaps, I was not surprised that day in May 1948 when the newspaper front pages carried reports of her suicide. After the *Daily Express* broke the story, the *Daily Mirror* took it up.

THE TRAGIC LOVE OF LADY JOAN COVENTRY

Lady Joan Blanche Coventry, 23, sister of the fourteen-year-old Earl of Coventry, fell in love with a married man. She tried to forget. Deciding on a business career, she went to Newbury (Berks) for a secretarial course at a commercial college. At the college – and at the Newbury hotel where she was found suffering from a fatal overdose of aspirin – she called herself Miss Joan Coventry.

The man with whom she was in love is not being called as a witness at today's inquest, according to the police last night. Colonel O.D. Smith, a relative of Lady Joan's mother, the Countess of Coventry, told the *Daily Mirror*: 'We all knew that Lady Joan was trying to get over a love affair. There was never a question of an engagement because the man she was in love with was already married. Three weeks ago, with the full knowledge of her mother, Lady Joan went to Newbury alone. She decided to take a commercial course at Newbury to become a secretary. She thought that would help her forget the tragedy of her love. Apparently she just could not forget.'

The Countess stayed last night at the hotel where her daughter was found dying. She will attend the inquest. One of the hotel staff said of Lady Joan: 'She always appeared to have some great worry. All she would do was to eat, read in the lounge and go to bed. She was always on her own and appeared most lonely. The only telephone calls she would receive were from her mother.'

It was, I thought, a terribly sad and lonely end to a young woman who – by the luck of breeding and aristocratic connections – might have had the world at her feet. I thought, too, of the old curse of the Deerhursts and the number of lives this had blighted for the Coventry family. And I also reflected that, in some way, the death of Lady Joan in a shabby little hotel, far away from the grandeur of her ancestral seat, marked the passing of an age. In just six years the once mighty had now fallen and become as mortal and as vulnerable as the rest of us. The war had, indeed, changed everything. Forever.

Chapter Fourteen

Envoi – 'I Can Rest Easy'

Last night I dreamed of Croome Court.

In the years since I left service I have rarely visited the house or the estate – though it is open to the public these days and guests are welcomed into its surviving rooms and parkland. But I had been there with my son Allan and his wife – now pensioners themselves – to help my fading memory conjure up the recollections of a long-ago age.

We have come a long way since I began this tale. And you, reader, what have you taken from my story? Has it been what you expected from someone who began her working life, as no more than a slip of a girl, in one of the greatest houses in the land and in the service of one of the oldest aristocratic families in England?

It has not, I think, been the sort of story that would have

255

fitted easily into the neat television dramas of life below stairs. I have tried to give you not just a sense of what it was like to be a lady's maid with the constant demands of tending to the needs of a Countess. I hope you have had some sense of what it meant to be one of the gentry in those long-ago days – and what it meant also to be called to be in their service. I also hope I have painted some colours into the fading picture of what life was – and what it meant – nearly 80 years ago.

For England was very different then. We were a nation – or, more accurately, two nations – of people who knew and understood their place in the scheme of things. And if that place was harsh and – as it undoubtedly was – unfair, the counterbalance to this social injustice was a sense of some stability: however restrictive the hierarchy and order of things, it was at least ordered and, with that, came a feeling of security even in the worst of economic times, when hunger was never far from our door.

We were a nation of churchgoers – as I have remained all of my life – and a people who had values and standards, which (whether wrong or right) we stuck to. Phrases from my childhood still come back to me. FHB is a particular one – it stood for Families Hold Back – and meant that, when guests came to eat at our table, it was they who filled their plates first (however meagre the rations) while we waited our turn.

I learned at my parents' knees to respect my elders, to listen to what they told me and never to answer back. And if that instruction was sometimes re-enforced with a clip to a youthful ear, I wonder really whether it did more good than harm. I see how family life has changed today – and not for the better – and struggle to understand how we got here in such a short passage of time.

Family life for people of my generation and of my class was all-important. It was the glue that held the nation together and, if it curtailed freedom, we at least learned that with rights come responsibilities and by the time you're ready to claim the former, well, you'd better be old and wise enough to accept the latter.

We learned, too, the value of thrift in an unforgiving world. We learned not to leave food on our plates because that was a waste which none of us could afford. We learned, in that famous wartime phrase, to make do and mend. And we learned to say – at least in public – 'mustn't grumble', even in times that gave us every excuse to do just that.

The land itself was different too. Britain was still much more in tune with the old, rural ways and the seasons were marked, as they had been for generations, with church services and an understanding of what each meant. It is, I know, a cliché but, in my little corner of England at least, crime was all but non-existent. Doors were never locked

– I can't remember bolting up my house at night until at least the early 1970s – even in the grandest of mansions. Going back to Croome, I noticed the little door underneath the big stone steps leading up to the house itself: on those occasions when I – often accompanied by Dorothy Clarke – had been out late, we would sneak back in though this entrance. It was never locked, no matter what the hour – although on more than one occasion Mr Latter might be patrolling the long echoing corridor that ran off it to the staircases at either end.

Why was this, I wonder? I think the answer must be that we had values then. Now, that, I'm sure, isn't a fashionable idea these days when there seems to be little agreement on what's wrong and what's right. Perhaps we saw things too much in black and white back then but today I fear we have lost sight even of the varying shades of grey, until everything is just a sort of white that's got indelibly grubby. When we saw wrong, we said so and called it what it was: today people seem just to wring their hands and say, 'We must talk about this or debate that,' and nothing gets done. Maybe it was our faith – and Lord knows as a nation we needed that during the war. Don't get me wrong, I'm not suggesting we should all start going to church again as we once did but maybe we could once again learn to live faithfully?

By contrast, I wonder how many of these lessons – and

how much of this code of behaviour – was either accepted or learned by those set above us in the social order. They, like us, knew their place and knew, as they knew that the sun rises in the east and sets in the west, that they were our 'betters'; that they were placed on this earth to lead and we to serve.

But we learned from our earliest years that life was a test and what mattered was the choices you made, never knowing whether you'd made the right one until it was too late: you might be right, you might be wrong but you had no option but to choose and, when all was said and done, you'd better be prepared to take the consequences. Did our masters and mistresses know that? I wonder.

The 1930s were, I know now, the dying embers of the once-glowing fires of the aristocracy. Generations upon generations had reaped the rewards from the social system of Britain but now the price of those rewards was being called in just as sure as the tallyman would call for the weekly instalments for purchases made on tick by the working classes. Death duties, the rising cost of maintaining vast 18th-century mansions and the willingness of each new generation to play more than it worked. Clogs to clogs in three generations was an old saying among my class of people and, if it took the gentry that I came to know a few more generations than that, well, it came to them in the end.

Only two of the Coventrys ever really came home to Croome after the war. In 1948 the Countess – my mistress – left the estate and I never heard a word from her ever again. Shortly afterwards the National Trust took over the house and the estate, and maintains its fading splendour as best as funds allow to this day. If you can, then do as I did recently: stand in the long, cold tunnel of the main servants' corridor, close your eyes and listen to the ghosts of those who served there. My eyes are old now and tired and my memory fades but, somehow, these walls and floors speak to me of days gone by: harder days, it is true, but better ones, I think. Days when, for all its faults, the country was a nation and the people who lived here knew that they were a part of it.

And when you have finished there – and heard, I hope, Mr Latter scolding a footman or teasing Winnie Sapstead about the quality of her cooking – follow my footsteps up the path that leads away from Croome Court and to the quiet church, set on a gentle rise where every Sunday I gave thanks for all that I received and prayed for the health and safety of all those I held dear.

Here on the wall you will find the evidence that the 10th Earl of Coventry came home, at least in spirit: a marble plaque bearing his name and the date of his death in service adding to the tombs and catafalques of his once-mighty predecessors. Stop a while here and breathe in the air of an age which is long past, a time which is now history, a people who – but for me – are gone (I hope) to a better place.

Then step out and, negotiating the little bushes and briars which surround the church walls now, look beyond the wooden fence and the stile that mark the boundaries of consecrated ground. There, resting quietly and unremarked, you will find the grave of Lady Joan Coventry. Perhaps here, above all else, is the most telling symbol of what once was and how all things change.

This has been my story, one of the rich and powerful and the ordinary folk who served them; it has been the story of a mansion but also that of the smaller, meaner homes of ordinary people. I am old now and tired. I need, I think, to ponder a little on the memories that telling this little tale has stirred. If my words and my life have served any purpose, perhaps it had been to remind you who we once were and how we once lived. And if it does, then, if I may say so, that is all to the good, for, if we forget these, we will lose sight of who we are now – rich or poor, high born or working class, the servant or the served. Then I, at last, can rest easy.